Bless His Soul

The Agony, The Ecstasy, & The Destiny of Michael Jackson

Bless His Soul

The Agony, The Ecstasy, & The Destiny of Michael Jackson

L. Roi Boyd III

KWE PUBLISHING, LLC
Prince George, Virginia

Copyright © 2018 Cultural Libations
All Rights Reserved
culturallibations@gmail.com

Boyd III, L. Roi
Bless His Soul: The Agony, The Ecstasy, and The Destiny of Michael Jackson

Copyright © 2018 by Cultural Libations
Original manuscript copyright by L. Roi Boyd III
Editors: Eric S. King, Kimberley Eley
Associate Editor: Rebekah L. Pierce
Cover Artwork by: Martha High
Graphics by: Selene Riddick
Photography by: Robert Lee Sims III and Danny Holcomb

ISBN (paperback) 978-1-7326273-4-5– ISBN (ebook) 978-1-7326273-5-2
Library of Congress Catalog Number 2017962950
All illustrations ©2017 Martha Harvin, used by permission
All memorabilia photographs ©2017, 2018 Danny Holcomb, used by permission
All Gary, Indiana photographs ©2017 Robert Lee Sims III, used by permission
The suppositions expressed in this manuscript are solely the suppositions based on the research and inferences of the author and do not represent the thoughts or opinions of the publisher.

Second Edition. All rights reserved. This book may not be reproduced in whole or in part without written permission from the publisher, except by reviewers who are hereby given the right to quote brief passages in a review. No part of the publication may be reproduced or transmitted in any form or by any means, electronic, mechanical, photocopying, recording, or otherwise without prior written permission from the publisher.

Although every precaution has been taken to verify the accuracy of the information contained herein, the author assumes no responsibility for any errors or omissions. The author shall have neither liability nor responsibility to any person or entity with respect to loss or damage caused, or alleged to have been caused, directly or indirectly, by the information contained in this book.
Printed in the United States of America

L. Roi Boyd III
639-F Westover Hills Blvd.
Richmond, VA 23225
(757) 285.2117
culturallibations@gmail.com

© 2018 Cultural Libations
All Rights Reserved

"'Bless His Soul' is a raw, in-depth look into the shaping of what would be Michael Jackson's finest, most earth-shattering moment as the world's greatest entertainer and artist. Many will never understand the level of commitment and sacrifice this musician had to make, especially navigating through a tough industry to find his lane and make his mark on music (by his own standards). Family is love and family can be tough. So breaking away was essential, but not easy when on the voyage of self-discovery. But he found himself, right? And with that, he made the world love, think, dream, sing, show compassion and dance like no other. Thanks Roi for showing this side of MJ."

~Christopher Barnes: Producer of Musiq Soulchild, Ledisi, and solo recording artist

"In 'Bless His Soul,' the author does a great job of chronicling the growth of Michael Jackson as a performer and writer during what he penned as the King of Pop's formative years (1975-1978). Having grown up with The Jackson 5, I started deejaying at 12 years old. What an unforgettable experience! The J5 were like The Beatles to the black community, appealing to fans from 8 to 80. If you're an MJ fan, as I am, get it! Great read!"

~Guy Brody, Veteran Radio & Television Personality

The Songs featured in this musicological study include:

"Blues Away"
© 1976 Mijac Music (BMI)

"Style Of Life"
© 1976 Rat Trap Music Publishing, Mijac Music (BMI)

"Push Me Away"
© 1978 Rat Trap Music Publishing, Siggy Music, Vabritmar Music, Mijac Music, Ran Jack Music (BMI)

"Things I Do For You"
© 1978 Rat Trap Music Publishing, Siggy Music, Vabritmar Music, Mijac Music, Ran Jack Music (BMI)

"Shake Your Body (Down To The Ground)"
© 1978 Rat Trap Music Publishing, Siggy Music, Vabritmar Music, Mijac Music, Ran Jack Music (BMI)

"Destiny"
© 1978 Rat Trap Music Publishing, Siggy Music, Vabritmar Music, Mijac Music, Ran Jack Music (BMI)

"Bless His Soul"
© 1978 Rat Trap Music Publishing, Siggy Music, Vabritmar Music, Mijac Music, Ran Jack Music (BMI)

"That's What You Get For Being Polite"
© 1978 Rat Trap Music Publishing, Siggy Music, Vabritmar Music, Mijac Music, Ran Jack Music (BMI)

"This is It"
©2009 Mijac Music/PaulAnne Music Incorporated. (BMI)
IQ Music Limited/Sony/ATV Music Publishing

Lyric transcriptions for "Blues Away" and "Style of Life" and "This Is It" have been found at the website http://www.azlyrics.com.

Lyric transcriptions for the songs on the Destiny album have been found in the lyric sheet included in the Destiny album package.

Musical Key Notations

Transcribed by JaCari Diggs, Department of Music, Virginia State University

Ex. 1 Things I Do For You

Ex. 2 Shake Your Body (Down To The Ground)

Ex. 3 Destiny

Ex. 4 Bless His Soul

Ex. 5 That's What You Get (For Being Polite)

Ex. 6 This Is It

Notice Of Fair Use

Under Sec. 107 of the Copyright Act of 1977, allowance is made for Fair Use of copyrighted materials for purposes such as criticism, comment, news reporting, teaching, scholarship, and research. Fair Use is a use permitted under statutory copyright law that might otherwise be infringed upon. The educational use purposes of this book qualify it under appropriate statutory law.

In good faith, the author attests that this manuscript contains Fair Use of short excerpts of copyrighted song lyrics for educational purposes.

This work contains original work of commentary and critical analysis. Quotations are attributed to the original composers, authors, writers, and sources.

TABLE OF CONTENTS

PREFACE 1

***DESTINY* ALBUM 40ᵀᴴ ANNIVERSARY EDITION NOTE** 5

INTRODUCTION 9

PROLOGUE: DESTINY, WEALTH, AND POWER
.... 21

CHAPTER ONE: THE JOURNEY TO DESTINY 31

CHAPTER TWO: PRE-DESTINY 63

CHAPTER THREE: MANIFEST DESTINY: THE AGONY AND THE ECSTASY BETWEEN THE NOTES (A MUSICOLOGICAL ANALYSIS OF THE *DESTINY* ALBUM) 73
BLAME IT ON THE BOOGIE 75
PUSH ME AWAY 83
THINGS I DO FOR YOU 97
SHAKE YOUR BODY (DOWN TO THE GROUND)
.... 107
DESTINY 121
BLESS HIS SOUL 135
ALL NIGHT DANCIN' 149
THAT'S WHAT YOU GET (FOR BEING POLITE) 163

CHAPTER FOUR: THIS IS IT: THE MUSICOLOGICAL CORRELATION BETWEEN "THIS IS IT" AND "BLESS HIS SOUL" 177
THIS IS IT 179

EPILOGUE: FULFILLED DESTINY 193

WORKS CITED **213**

APPENDIX **223**

To Booster, whose Jackson Five collection enlightened me to see that pop music is more than just...pop music.

And to Yemaja, your feedback showed me that I could do this and anything. Thank You. I Love You.

"Every single being has an unfulfilled destiny."
--Rev. Dr. Michael Bernard Beckwith

Preface

This book is about the coming of age of Michael Jackson and how the events in his life between 1975 and 1978 were lyrically verbalized and musically communicated in The Jacksons' 1978 album entitled *Destiny*. This is a musicological study that includes an abundance of analytical commentary. Lyrical quotations of the composer are necessary and incorporated as they provide support to the themes and arguments expressed in this work as well as transcribed musical keys.

"Bless His Soul: The Agony, the Ecstasy, & the Destiny of Michael Jackson" is an examination of how Jackson processed and documented his human experience during a tumultuous period in his life that eventually gave birth to his superstar status and his greatest work five years later (*Thriller*). For musicians, musicologists, and studio professionals, this manuscript should only be an accompaniment to the playing of the songs on the *Destiny* album.

This manuscript is not an attempt to be an authoritative evaluation on the music of The Jacksons and Michael Jackson as the suppositions are merely the inferences of the author as the result of research and analysis. When all is said and done Jackson's eccentricities and lifestyle choices do not matter. What he wanted people to focus on and remember him by more than anything else was his music. He deserves a critical review as much as Tchaikovsky or Prokofiev.

In a May 1992 interview with Ebony Magazine, Michael discussed his *Dangerous* album with associate publisher and executive editor of Jet magazine Robert E. Johnson. In speaking to the creative process in the application of that album, what he said is appurtenant to his entire body of work. Jackson stated, "I would like to see children and teenagers and parents and all races all over the world, hundreds and hundreds of years from now, still pulling out songs and dissecting it. I want it to live."

L. Roi Boyd, III, MA, MFA
Richmond, VA
December 2017

Destiny Album 40th Anniversary Edition Note

It is a great pleasure to present this 2nd edition of *Bless His Soul: The Agony, The Ecstasy & The Destiny of Michael Jackson.* This volume is especially important to me as it commemorates the 40th anniversary of a work that ushered the coming of age of not only an American musical dynasty but of a musical icon who would eventually become arguably, the greatest entertainer in the world and produce the greatest selling album of all time.

Many regard *Destiny* as the Jacksons' greatest album and there is a story to that, as we will examine here. Not only will we explore the events that led to The Jacksons' masterpiece but we will examine within the music, in a musicological fashion, the structure of hit songs like "Shake Your Body (Down To The Ground)" and memorable album tracks like "That's What You Get For Being Polite". However, to understand who Michael Jackson was, we take a historical inspection of his life between 1975 and

1978 coupled with the musicological factors in my research to comprehend the result of seven wonderfully composed songs and the production of one of the landmark rhythm and blues/disco albums of the 1970's.

It is very fitting that we acknowledge the 40th anniversary of *Destiny* in 2018. For it is this year that not only do we acknowledge the 40th anniversary of this album, we also remember the 30th anniversary of Michael Jackson as the first recording artist in world history to have five number one singles from a single album (*BAD*); the 50th anniversary of The Jacksons in the mainstream music industry; approximately the 70th anniversary of Joseph Jackson's eponymous blues band, The Falcons, which will fuel the vision of what would become The Jackson 5; and had he lived, Michael Jackson would have turned 60 years old.

It is my hope that musicologists and Jackson aficionado's will acquire a greater understanding of the music and the artist as an alternative perspective to the tainted mainstream gaze. I wish to thank all of you for your support in this endeavor in the last year and for your continued support to come. Thank you very much. "I Love You More".

L. Roi Boyd, III, MA, MFA
Richmond, VA
December 2018

8

Introduction

"What happened to Michael Jackson?" In the last 25 years of his life, public concerns were not entirely aimed towards his music, but more toward his changing appearance and personal life. In the late 1980's, there was talk and concern of him looking pale in that there was a deliberate attempt to lighten the pigmentation of his skin. This, along with his many plastic surgeries, led many to believe this was an effort to erase his African-American features, and gave the subtle context that he was in pursuit of a more Caucasian image. In addition, what fueled this perspective were the bizarre lifestyle choices; namely, wearing surgical masks in public, insisting that his children wear masks to conceal their identities, and publicly venting his anger towards the press and critics through his song lyrics.

Although it is true that Jackson made some peculiar choices in his behavior, the disastrous consequence was that his private life received more press than his music in the last two decades of his life. Once known as a genius, by the end of the 20th Century, he was commonly known as "Wacko Jacko," a circus freak show and, to many in the African-American community, a poster boy for self-hatred. However, what's interesting, and what many have failed to grasp, is that while Jackson's skin became lighter and whiter, the music became "blacker and blacker." *Dangerous* was a New Jack Swing masterpiece and an historical document of its time, while *HIStory: Past, Present, and Future Book 1,* was a Hip Hop extravaganza that featured the likes of The Notorious B.I.G. and Shaquille O'Neal. Moreover, Invincible was an Urban/"Hip Hop/R&B" affair thanks to the production styling of Rodney Jerkins. Beneath the public "train wreck" that his personal life had become, Jackson was becoming, musically, more and more of an "OG" (Original Gangsta), still hip in his execution of the current Hip-Hop musical styles, while also serving as an influence on younger performers such as Usher and Justin Timberlake.

Jackson was a complicated man who lived a complicated life, not necessarily so because he did not have a childhood due to excessive performing and traveling, but because of the pressures that came with being a lead singer of a very successful group as a teenager. Michael bore a huge weight by carrying an entire show every night and promoting both albums and a public image that involved a support-team of competent personnel. The lead singer carries all the responsibility that can make or break the connection between the group and the audience. Keith Richards calls this "Lead Singer Syndrome" and he felt sorry for all the weight Mick Jagger had to carry. As opposed to Jagger, who carried it as a grown man, Jackson had carried this responsibility since the age of 11, when The Jackson Five made their American debut on "The Ed Sullivan Show" in 1969. By the time Michael was 17, he was growing creatively restless and eager to express himself. This self-initiative was nearly impossible because both the forces of Motown Records and his father, Joseph Jackson, would dictate the direction of his creativity for at least another three years. Between the ages of 17 to 24, Jackson was finding himself, these were his "turbulent years" (1975-1982); and he documented the experiences in various songs, through an album aptly titled *Destiny*, which was the third album under The Jacksons' contract with CBS/Epic Records.

    It is safe to say now that the *Destiny* album saved their careers. Michael Jackson played a pivotal role in co-writing nearly every song on the album. He channeled his problems in a creative vortex through this album. Lyrically, this album discloses the desire of becoming closer to family, the frustration of giving all of himself to others without receiving anything in return, exploitation by employees and family, the increasing dissatisfaction of working with family and recognizing, feeling, and facing the urge to strike out on his own.

    In early June 2009, I had been thinking about the Jacksons, knowing that Michael was in rehearsal for his upcoming "This Is It" tour. I decided to put on the *Destiny* album just for the pleasure of listening; I also felt the need to take the lyric sheet and follow along as I listened. Halfway through listening to the album and reading the lyrics, it was revealed to me that Jackson had been crying for help since the late 1970's, years before *Thriller*. Clearly, anyone who wanted to know what happened to Michael Jackson merely had to listen to the lyrics of this album. Michael's problems did not materialize after the success of *Thriller*. The trouble with *Thriller* was that the mania made his problems worse and magnified his personal life to a level that he never experienced before as a public figure. Three weeks after my listening session, Jackson passed away. I remember thinking: of someone who wished to be understood by many through his music; would anyone take the time to learn and study the true man through his creativity?

    In the middle of a "Michael Jackson summer," the likes that which have not been experienced in this country since 1984, I proposed a lecture with the Black History Museum and Cultural Center of Richmond, VA, that would kick off a three-and-a-half-month-long exhibit of Jackson memorabilia that I would curate (I have been a collector of Jackson memorabilia for over 30 years). The public reaction to the lecture was so positive; many people have told me that it should be the basis for a class. I could not see that as a possibility; however, it was easier to see the lecture as a potential book. Here we are eight years later with this publication, and my desire is to share it with the world and to raise awareness of this work in the Jackson oeuvre, for the younger generation.

    Now that The Jacksons are back on the road touring again, understanding their work from an intensive perspective than entertainment is musically important, as they are not only carrying on the legacy of a seven-decade musical dynasty but they are also carrying the legacy of their brother, who broke racial and cultural boundaries by bringing people together through his art; this is their story as well.

This book is not a linear biography, it is an analytical commentary. Musical notations are included to further make the case that emotion is not only translated in words, but also through music. A great companion in the analysis of this material was Rita Steblin's "A History of Key Characteristics in the 18th and Early 19th Centuries." Written notation expresses the state of mind of the composer. I found this insight necessary when investigating the life and music of Michael Jackson.

As we are examining *Destiny*, the album, portions of the album's lyrics are quoted and the songs will be examined in their sequential order to possess a clear picture of my hypothesis. My argument is as follows: That Jackson was suffering with the internal turmoil of his transition from a child star to an adult, while carrying the weight of responsibility of keeping a family group together simply by his position as its most visible member as the lead singer while also coping with the overwhelming need to express himself individually without his brothers.

The writing and production of this album was truly his expression and release. These internal problems, prophetically manifest themselves through his behavior later in the 1980's and 90's.

According to the Best Practices in the Fair Use of Copyrighted Materials in Music Scholarship, published by the American Musicological Society, "Reasonable care should be taken to ensure that no more of a lyric is quoted than the critical or scholarly context requires: however, this admonition permits a very wide variance in the actual length of quoted material, as long as the quoted material is necessary to the argument being made."[i]

Let us understand that the findings in this book are my suppositions based on the conclusions of my analysis through historical research, supported by various sources of print and electronic media, through historical events and interviews given by Dr. Jackson (LHD, Honoris Causa, Fisk University, 1988), his mother Katherine, and others. J. Randy Taraborrelli's book, "Michael Jackson: The Magic and the Madness" (1991), was a substantial read in the life and career of Jackson. Other musicological texts such as Sir James Jeans' Science & Music, which featured excerpts from Hermann Von Helmholtz's book on the physics of music theory, Tonempfindungen was consulted and many other sources which are found in the bibliography page at the end of this book. Also included are the lyrical and musical content of the album compilation, based on my perspective that the album serves as a diary of the primary composer, Michael Joseph Jackson. The quotation of lyrics is strictly for the scholarly context for this book. The reader may take what she or he likes and leave the rest.

    I would like to acknowledge those persons who played an important part in the production of this book: particularly Dr. Maureen Elgersman Lee and Mary Lauderdale who worked with me on the Jackson exhibit and lecture in 2009. Keith Wallace for his help in the music transcriptions. JaCari Diggs for transcribing the musical keys, and Russell Wilson, Clarence Page, and Brenda Dabney

Nichols, for their support. Great thanks also goes out to Ms. April Spears at Virginia State University who helped "rescue" the manuscript one night (I am greatly appreciative), Sam Beason, Jenna Shepherd, Susan Moncure, Charles Moreland, Sr., and Charles Moreland, Jr., for their irrefutable feedback in reading pages of the manuscript; Kevin Harris for additional musical examination; Lina Kim for being instrumental in the graphic design of the cover; my consultation committee members, Dorothy Rowley, Ramona Leigh Taylor, Reginald Small, Sharon Loving, and Amos Richardson for helping me acquire a different perspective on the work. Furthermore, tremendous thanks go out to my impeccable editors Eric S. King and Rebekah L. Pierce, who helped me articulate my thoughts in a way that is most pleasing to the tongue and easy for the reader to understand; my publisher Kim Wells Eley for her undying support and believing in me and this project; Martha High for her beautiful artwork, thank you for your help and friendship; and of course to Yemaja Jubilee, whose constructive criticism and encouragement, inspired me to "tidy it up" and put it out! Thank You.

    The arts are a mirror of man; they provide our identity and help us determine our individual culture. Jackson's work is worthy of an intensive historical biographical analysis just as the masters of Renaissance art, Elizabethan writers and the French Impressionists (just to name a few) have been studied. Michael Jackson is arguably the greatest entertainer in the history of the world. His legacy will be felt, studied, and quoted from for the longevity of human civilization. As the scholar C. Liegh McInnis once wrote, "we must understand that popular art is a gauge or a barometer for society. When we study popular artists, we are innately studying the periods of the artists which give us a better understanding of our history and of humanity." [ii]Artists, through their work, help us to acquire a greater understanding of ourselves; and as it appears to be with Jackson, arguably, the greatest entertainer of his time, this history, these lyrics, and this music was his Destiny.

20

Prologue: Destiny, Wealth, and Power

"Go west young man and grow up with the country" were the words written in an editorial by Presbyterian minister and newspaper editor John Babsone Lane Soule. [iii] The essay was published in an 1851 issue of the Terre Haute, Indiana Express. History later attributes the quote to an 1865 editorial in the New York Tribune written by Horace Greeley. Greeley, a member of the U.S. House of Representatives from New York's 6th district, supported westward expansion. He saw the fruitful, rich farmland of the west as a blessing of opportunity for the eastern American to work hard, reap the benefits of his success and to make something of himself. Greeley wrote,

> **Washington is not a fit place to live in. The rents are high, the food is bad, the dust is disgusting, and the morals are deplorable. Go west, young man and grow up with the country.[iv]**

With a new America on the verge of rebirth after a tumultuous civil war, ex-soldiers from both sides of the conflict took up many professions; among these were sales clerks, mechanics, jewelers, men with a new sense of enterprise who possessed the expectation of great personal success that had never been previously experienced. It was the birth of a new national concept, the realization of a dream in achieving personal individual success that can only be found in America and creating a legacy where one can give their children more than they had while growing up.

Regardless of who coined the phrase "Go West young man," the idea of moving westward and taking advantage of the 1862 homestead act was more than appealing. The ideology that white settlers were justified and destined to expand westward across North America was known as Manifest Destiny. It was believed that it was, "the virtue of the American people and their institutions to expand westward; that it was the mission of the American people to spread these institutions, thereby redeeming and remaking the world in the image of the

United States, and it is the destiny under God to do this work."[v]

The possibility of creating a racial utopia was a factor in a time when the Caucasian race believed themselves to be superior and separate from all other races. This credence warranted racial slavery as well as the larceny of Native American lands and their genocide. With the completion of the transcontinental railroad on May 10, 1869, the expansion of the west was considered complete and Americans have manifested their destiny....well, maybe not all Americans.

"More than 100 negroes were lynched the first year of the twentieth century. By 1915 the grand total had reached 1,100!"[vi] The reestablishment of a terror organization movement known as the Ku Klux Klan used violence to suppress the upward mobility of African Americans in the American south. When America became involved in the first world war in 1917, "seven million of the nation's eight million African Americans resided below the Cotton Curtain. But over the next fifteen years, more than one-tenth of the country's black population would voluntarily move north, this exodus will be known as The Great Migration. The first wave of this journey lasted until 1930, it was the first step in the full nationalization of the African-American population."[vii]

Southern life for the American Negro was hopeless. Sharecropping hardly provided any means of economic stability and with the boll weevil infestations destroying the southern cotton industry in the 1920's, sharecroppers and laborers were forced to find other forms of employment. The great flood of 1913 demolished the farms and homes of those who lived along the banks of the Mississippi river; many of these farmers and residents were African Americans. Seven decades earlier, Soule encouraged white Americans to go west; now with no public encouragement needed, African Americans simply knew that it was their time to go. The big cities of New York, Philadelphia, St. Louis, Detroit, Pittsburgh, Indianapolis, and Chicago were the primary destinations for greater opportunity in reliable, steady employment. "Labor shortages in northern factories due to World War I resulted in thousands of jobs available to African Americans in railroads, meatpacking plants, automobile industry, and steel mills."[viii]

As Chicago was one of the primary destinations of southern transients in the great migration, the size of the metropolis could be overwhelming as much as the job market. Many African Americans resided nearby in small towns like East Chicago and Gary, both located in neighboring Indiana. But even in these more manageable areas the employment outlook was dim.

Economic opportunities did not keep pace with educational progress. Negroes continued to be barred from skilled occupations and, regardless of their qualifications and ambitions, were relegated for the most part to menial, unskilled, low-paying jobs. Socially there was almost no mingling of the races, and Negroes were denied accommodations in most public places which white patrons frequented in spite of the adoption of an innocuous civil rights law.

In the social and economic realms, there was evidence that barriers were hardening rather than relaxing at the end of the 19th century and that race feeling was stronger than it had been a few years earlier.[ix]

It appeared that any migrant who bought the myth of racial tolerance in the American North was soon to be disappointed. The post-civil war paradigm of a racist southern landscape and a northern utopia where merit was based on individual character rather than skin color is a misconception. Although Jim Crow was not blatantly present in the northern states, racism, whether northeastern or mid-western, was more systematic. Indiana's white population tended to hold the beliefs (similar to Southern whites) that African Americans were inferior and this alone was the nucleus behind the rigid racial boundaries that existed economically, politically, and socially.

One way for an ambitious black man to find his way out of the poverty and strife of the Jim Crow south was to go north and take a job in the steel mills.

By 1950 Negroes [in Indiana] numbered 175,785 or 4.4 per cent of the whole. The new arrivals headed for the industrial centers, by-passing the older Ohio River communities and moving northward to Indianapolis and the newer cities in the extreme north, especially the steel centers in the Gary. [x]

Sharon Zulkin, in her book, "Landscapes of Power: From Detroit to Disney World," wrote, "steel has power because it has been the lifeline in industrial society."[xi] It exuded a powerful and firm association between strength and community. Zulkin goes on to say that, "Long before steel was produced by capital and labor in giant, steaming mills, it combined alchemy, destiny, wealth, and power."[xii] Elements that beheld a 20-year-old steel crane operator from Fountain Hill, Arkansas who dreamed of going to California to find his destiny in the arena of golden gloves boxing. His name was Joseph Walter Jackson.

A high school dropout and the product of divorced parents, Joseph moved with his father to Oakland, California. After his father married his third wife, he reunited with his mother in East Chicago, Indiana where he became a crane operator at Inland steel. He pursued boxing and with his brother Luther formed a blues band and played gigs in the local area. It was there in East Chicago where he met 17-year-old Katherine Scruse at a neighborhood dance. "When Katherine met Joe she fell for him immediately. He married someone else but the marriage lasted only a year."[xiii] After Joseph's marriage ended in divorce, the two courted and began a six-month engagement. "When they were courting, the two would snuggle up together on cold winter nights and sing Christmas carols. Sometimes they would harmonize, and the blend was a good one, thanks to Katherine's beautiful soprano voice. Michael Jackson [felt] he inherited his singing ability from his mother."[xiv]

The two would often share their dreams and divulge the course of their individual dreams with each other. Katherine aspired to become a nurse, although she really wanted to be an actress and a country-western singer. Joseph dreamed of destiny, wealth, and power. The acquisition of personal destiny as a self-made man pulling himself up by his bootstraps out of poverty, earning the freedom of financial wealth and the power to make things happen in his life outside of the usual responsibilities of food, clothing, and shelter. With a strong determination, Joseph made plans to move to California and make it as a professional boxer. Soon, when Katherine was pregnant, Joseph Jackson's destiny made a turn from California to Gary, Indiana. Like the blocks of steel, he moved on the crane he operated, he and Katherine would formulate the genesis of the destiny, wealth, and power they dreamed of. Through their union and the raising of their nine children, they will develop and manifest their dreams into reality and ultimately produce a musical dynasty.

Chapter One: The Journey to Destiny

In the 1950's, the cold war commenced between the Soviet Union and the United States. Television, which first reached the marketplace in the previous decade, reached a new progression as most Americans owned a TV set by the end of the decade. Classic crooners like Frank Sinatra, Johnnie Ray, and Patti Page were curtailed by a new kind of music fusing rhythm and blues and country-western that will come to be known as rock and roll. And in Gary, Indiana, Joseph Jackson became the patriarch of a large family residing at 2300 Jackson Street, Gary, Indiana.

The Jackson Family home at 2300 Jackson Street, Gary, Indiana

"He had no choice but to work in the mills. Almost every African-American man in the Gary region did back then."[xv] Joseph struggled to provide for his family through the meager existence of the four o'clock to midnight shift of Inland Steel in East Chicago, Indiana [xvi] and U.S. Steel in Gary[xvii]. "Whenever Joseph was laid off, he found work harvesting potatoes, and during these periods the family would fill up on potatoes, boiled, fried, or baked."[xviii] Jackson understood that if one can have a stable family then a stable economic income must come into the home. By the time Joseph and Katherine's seventh child, Michael, was born in 1958, "roughly twenty dollars a week [was added] to the family budget from Katherine's part time job as a cashier for Sears & Roebuck in Downtown Gary."[xix] The young couple fed, clothed, and raised their nine children in a small, two bedroom, brick-and-aluminum sided home about a hundred feet deep and fifty feet wide. Looking back, Joseph Jackson remarked, "Something inside of me told me there was more to life than this. What I really wanted more than anything was to find a way into the music business."ˣˣ A strict disciplinarian, Jackson was distant and showed little affection, traits he acquired from his father while growing up in Arkansas. When discovering the musical talent possessed by their sons Jackie (b.1951), Tito (b.1953), Jermaine (b.1954), Marlon (b.1957), and Michael (b.1958), Jackson encouraged, worked, honed and cultivated their talent. The family quintet performed in talent shows and nightclubs around the greater Gary and Chicago area, and later along the "chitlin' circuit," the name given to a string of performance venues in the Eastern, Southern, and Upper Mid-West areas of the United States that were considered safe for African American entertainers to perform during the era of racial segregation in the early to mid-20th Century.

On July 25, 1968, the boys were signed to Motown Records, 14 months after being discovered by Gladys Knight and Bobby Taylor (from Bobby Taylor and the Vancouvers) at the Apollo Theater amateur night competition, which the boys won. Taylor later invited the boys to open for himself and the Vancouvers at a concert in Chicago's Regal Theater. Impressed with their talent and showmanship, he became instrumental in introducing them to Berry Gordy for their audition. This introduction would become the start of a musical legacy that would change popular music forever[xxi].

    Exploding on the American scene on October 14, 1969, with the release of the single, "I Want You Back," Motown founder and president Berry Gordy promised the boys that their first four singles would become four consecutive number one hits. He kept good on that promise. "I Want You Back" was followed by "ABC," "The Love You Save," and "I'll Be There." Between 1970 and 1975, The Jackson 5 sold 39,200,000 albums, released 18 top 40 singles and embarked on three national tours and two world tours.

    In fulfilling their obligations to Motown, the brothers, under the management of Papa Joe, matured in their creativity. Privately, they had been writing, arranging, and producing their own material (under the Motown umbrella, such creativity would never have been brought forward, let alone accepted). Berry Gordy believed that the group would maintain their best sound by having session musicians and in-house songwriters and producers contribute material to their records. This conviction might have been supported when they first signed as an unpolished group in 1969, but by 1974, the boys were groomed musicians with a burning intensity to create, especially within Michael.

On May 15, 1975, Motown released The Jackson 5's ninth studio album, *Moving Violation*.[xxii] The lead single, a cover of The Supremes' 1968 hit single, "Forever Came Today," was the label's hope of a follow-up to the success of the group's previous smash hit, "Dancing Machine," released the previous year, which peaked at number two on the Billboard Hot 100 Chart. "Forever Came Today" peaked at number 60 on the U.S. Billboard chart and peaked at number six on the Billboard R & B chart. With the rise of Disco and the new stream of number one hits from acts in the likes of The Captain and Tennille, Van McCoy, and K.C. &

the Sunshine Band, The Jackson 5 were left in the dust.

With their last number one hit in 1970, The Jackson 5 had enough of Motown and the lack of creative support by the company. In the spring of 1975, Joe Jackson was shopping around for a new record deal and happened upon an interested CBS Records. Making matters more complicated, Jermaine Jackson was now married to Berry Gordy's daughter, Hazel. This situation was not easy for Jermaine who felt caught between his new wife and the changing tide of his family; in the end, he had to make a weighty decision.

Later that spring, Joe Jackson summoned Jermaine to the family's Hayvenhurst estate in Encino, California. When Jermaine arrived inside his parents' master bedroom, he saw four recording contracts signed and laying on the bed. Joe ordered Jermaine to sign the fifth contract, but Jermaine refused; the father and son fought and Jermaine left the group. Previously, younger brother Randy had made special guest appearances with the group but now, at the age of 14, he was brought in as a full-fledged member to replace Jermaine. With the new configuration of the group, now to be known as "The Jacksons," the group forged ahead with television appearances and concerts.

On Monday, June 30, 1975, Joseph Jackson arranged a press conference at the Rainbow Grill atop Rockefeller Center in New York City with the entire family sans Jermaine. This conference was to announce the family's new association with CBS; the absence of Jermaine was far from subtle. The press repeatedly asked if he would be joining the group with the label change. Joseph responded with a cagey "yes" and immediately took other questions.

In August of 1975, Michael Jackson would turn 17 years old. For six years, he had performed in the public eye in not only the guise of an entertainer, but also as a teen idol. For most of his life, Jackson had to be "on" at all times. By the mid-1970's, Jackson found that when people would notice him or see him up close, they became surprised or disappointed because he was no longer the little boy America had fallen in love with. He was an adolescent male. Part of Jackson's self-conscious concerns was his bout with acne and loneliness. Of this time, Jackson remarked,

> **I had very few close friends at the time and felt very isolated. I was so lonely that I used to walk through my neighborhood hoping I'd run into somebody I could talk to and perhaps become friends with. I wanted to meet people who didn't know who I was. I wanted to run into somebody who would be my friend because they liked me and needed a friend too, not because I was who I am. I wanted to meet anybody in the neighborhood—the neighborhood kids, anybody.** [xxiii]

This loneliness along with the ever-increasing yearning to express the music inside him only to find that there was a block to prevent him from doing so (Motown), Jackson found himself in a depression, fighting an agony that left little room for ecstasy.

Contributing to these personal problems was the burden Michael bore as the lead singer; his family was increasingly depending on him to help chart the direction the group should take with their mounting and encompassing business decisions. In May of 1975, Michael met with Gordy in an attempt to convince him to allow he and his brothers to take charge of their work. The meeting was unsuccessful and Gordy spoke to Michael in anger, insisting that the group would be better off with in-house writers and producers. Although Michael did not want to leave Motown, he sided with his father and the family because he knew that the move was in the group's best interest.

But the group still had eight months left on their Motown contract. Gordy was not happy that the boys signed with another label while still held under contractual obligations to Motown and felt that this was the ultimate act of treason from an artist. Because of this, Motown executive Tony Jones sent a memo to Joe Jackson requesting that the group return to the studio at once to record a new Jackson 5 album. Joseph refused.

Although the brothers could not record a note with CBS until the spring of '76, they spent the interim fulfilling their first obligation to CBS by taping four episodes for The Jacksons television variety show. More episodes were expected to come. Motown placed the group on "suspension" and filed a lawsuit against Joseph Jackson, The Jackson 5, and CBS for $5 million dollars in damages. The brothers gave their depositions in the beginning of 1976. When it was all over, the group officially left the company at the end of their contract, which expired on March 10, 1976. They were finally able to enter the studio to record an album that, for the first time, would feature their original compositions. Berry Gordy won the lawsuit by retaining the name "The Jackson 5," but he was only able to collect $600,000.00 in damages.[xxiv]

Meanwhile, Joseph Jackson became quite impressed with Epic Records largely because of their support for Black artists. What attracted him the most was the production team of Kenneth Gamble and Leon Huff. Pioneers of the "Philadelphia Sound" and the founders of Philadelphia International Records, Gamble & Huff's track record of hits were performed by the premier soul artists of the time: MFSB, The Three Degrees and Harold Melvin, and The Blue Notes. Joseph appreciated the company's commitment to Black music and approved of Gamble and Huff as producers while the boys honed their production skills.

The president of Epic at the time, Ron Alexenburg, and the director of Artists and Repertoire, Steve Popovitch, saw something special in the group, but felt that Motown had not tapped their full potential. As far as Alexenburg was concerned, the Jackson 5 had not really begun. Joseph Jackson was most concerned about seizing the opportunity for his sons to write and produce their own records. However, Walter Yetnikoff, the president of Epic's parent company, CBS Records, refused to allow the brothers to have creative control because he felt that the boys needed more work in perfecting their craft in songwriting and production. Although demo recordings of their work were presented to demonstrate their abilities, Yetnikoff was still unimpressed; in addition to forbidding the brothers to have artistic control, he also forbade them to choose material from other professional songwriters.

The brothers now found themselves in a similar situation that had compelled them to leave Motown. Yetnikoff's reasoning was that the group, while at Motown, had not developed a strong composition or production record of accomplishments that indicated that they had any potential in this area. Alexenburg had assured Joe Jackson, in an unwritten deal, that the brothers could choose three songs per album by accomplished composers; moreover, if they could write three good songs, then those songs would be given reasonable consideration. [xxv]

Shortly after the expiration of their Motown contract, the Jackson brothers reported to the Sigma Sound Recording Studios at 212 N.12th St. in Philadelphia, Pennsylvania, to record their first album after leaving Motown. The self-titled album, *The Jacksons*, was released on November 6, 1976[xxvi] under the joint label listing of Epic & Philadelphia International Records. A milestone for the group the album spawned a major hit, "Enjoy Yourself," which peaked at number six on the Billboard pop chart and number two on the Billboard R & B chart. Another hit single, which was more successful in the U.K., was "Show You the Way to Go." A quintessential representation of the Philadelphia sound, "Show You" reached number 6 on the R & B chart in America and number 28 on the Billboard Pop chart. While in Britain, it became the group's first number one hit.

Although the Gamble & Huff produced album was known as a production from the renowned duo, it also featured other staff producers from Philadelphia International. Dexter Wansel produced "Keep On Dancing," Gene McFadden, John Whitehead, and veteran soul songwriter, Victor Carstarphen, produced "Strength of One Man," and for the first time, the Jacksons penned two compositions. The first published and recorded composition by Michael Jackson entitled, "Blues Away" (produced by Gamble & Huff/McFadden and Whitehead/Dexter Wansel and The Jacksons) and the Tito and Michael collaboration "Style of Life" (produced by Gamble & Huff/McFadden and Whitehead and The Jacksons).

"Blues Away" is a short song, clocking at three minutes and twelve seconds that signals the emergence of a composer and producer. The song is not only about overcoming a deep depression, but also letting a young girl know that no matter how hard she may try to appease and seduce him, she will not succeed in taking his "blues away." Obviously personal, Jackson would later comment on his relationships with women and how they would come to help him deal with his depression.

> **Many girls want to know what makes me tick —why I live the way I live or do the things I do— trying to get inside my head. They want to rescue me from loneliness, but they do it in such a way that they give me the**

> **impression they want to share my loneliness, which I wouldn't wish on anybody, because I believe I'm one of the loneliest people in the world**[xxvii]

"Blues Away" chronicles the depression Jackson suffered as a teenager. This depression could have been rooted in loneliness, a changing family structure (the leaving of Motown and exit of Jermaine), and the adjustment to the world's changing perceptions that he was no longer a child star but also that he had disappointed the public by growing up. Later, Jackson would say that with "Blues Away," he was "going for the Jackie Wilson, 'Lonely Teardrops' way of laughing on the outside to stop the churning inside."[xxviii] The song is a simple, soulful R & B piano hook fused with a bluesy element. The piano, guitar and bass are in tight harmony in the gateway portion of the intro that leads to the full instrumental interlude, which then becomes complete with the congas and a luscious string section. Dexter Wansel adds a nice brass section that "walks" along with the piano's basic structure while Gamble & Huff produce the brass and strings to work together as a unit. Jackson's voice is reverbed to achieve a double tracked overdub effect. What is also interesting about Jackson's song is his new vocal sound. *The Jacksons* album is now remembered today partly because of the maturation of Michael's vocals from Motown.

Throughout the album, we hear Michael and the brothers mature as singers, and as we come to "Blues Away," located at the end of the record's first side, we find more versatility to Michael's voice. He tends to approach the song from the head register to maintain his high vocal range. Another tactic is his vocal affectations, original, distinct vocal sounds that are noted as a trademark in an artist's performing style. As early as 1974 with the Motown album, *G.I.T.: Get It Together*, Michael started to cultivate a new vocal style that would eventually become his trademark; more specifically, he would accentuate the downbeat with a vocal punch, and thus creating an original vocal percussive style.

Motown, being as controlling as they were with the group's sound, forbade Michael from continuing with the style. His vocal gymnastics alone is part of the reason "Blues Away" is symbolic of the group's newfound artistic independence. The first time we hear this kind of affectation on *The Jacksons* is in this song; the affectation occurs on the 12th measure, after the beginning piano introduction, completed with the bass and guitar licks that create the gateway into the song.

> **I'd like to be yours tomorrow/**
> **So I'm giving you some time to/**
> **think it over today/But-TA!/**
> **You can't take my Blues Away/**
> **No matter what you say babe**
>
> **--M. Jackson**[xxix]

"But-TA!" is the first affectation of a vocal sound that we will hear from an 18-year-old Michael Jackson, as he is carving his own sound. Throughout the song, we hear Jackson wanting to accentuate those notes through which he is gliding through, but instead, we hear him breathe somewhat rhythmically. This metrical breath can be heard counts before the second repeat of the chorus on the 16th measure on the 2nd & 3rd beats. "Blues Away" is one of the songs on the album's first side that breaks away from the Gamble & Huff positive message formula of music and dance overcoming sorrow. Jackson once referred to this "formula" designed by the producers for the group:

> **We knew that the message to promote peace and let music take over was a good one, but again it was more like the old O'Jays' "Love Train" and not really our style.**[xxx]

Befitting, in a macabre sense, is that the first original composition and production that we hear from the group is a song about overcoming depression. Also significant is that the principal composer, the one suffering from the blues, is the one who, at the time, was the spokesperson of the family and the most visible member. The family unit is a network of relationships within the social institution and within familial relationships, individuals will experience incoherence or fragmentation. Depression, no matter how chronic, is an illness. This fragmentation Jackson was experiencing is the antithesis of healing. "Healing requires relationships—relationships which lead to trust, hope, and a sense of being known." [xxxi] Maybe the destiny, wealth, and power that Joe Jackson desired for his family as a crane operator in Gary, Indiana, ten years earlier had taken its toll on his seventh son.

The closing song on the album, "Style Of Life," carries with it the strains of soul music that can be found in a Blaxploitation movie. Written by Tito and Michael, "Style Of Life," musically, summarizes the group's CBS debut as a mature band who has dropped their bubblegum sound in favor for an urbanized, soul aesthetic. As with much of the second portion of the album, "Style Of Life" possesses a strong presence of the congas as it accompanies a funky rhythm section pushed along by a hard driving bass, which we can safely presume was architected by Tito. With MFSB (the Philadelphia

International session band) as the musicians following the production lead of Gamble and Huff, McFadden and Whitehead, Dexter Wansel and The Jacksons, the song was able to stand strong with the nurturing and care of its ten producers.

Lyrically, Michael was clearly confronting the issues he and his family were facing. He writes in the character of a man in a failing relationship who tells his woman that because of her "wishy washy" controlling ways, he has no other option but to leave her and warns her that she must change her style of life.

> **Here I am reaching out for ya/**
> **But there's nothing to reach for.**
> **'Cause my mind don't believe**
> **what my eyes have seen/the**
> **blames you gave/**
> **You know (You know)/**
> **and I know nobody wants you**
> **with your/**
> **wishy, washy ways/**
> **I have tried to make you change**
> **but you remain the same And I**
> **feel/**
> **you really come to nothing,**
> **no.**[xxxii]

Who was Michael really speaking to in this song? Was he talking to himself? During that turbulent period, there were days when Michael wanted to stay at Motown and there were days where he felt that he needed to leave. Was he talking to Jermaine about leaving the group? On the other hand, was he speaking to Berry Gordy? Gordy is a wise hypothesis based on the bridge where he writes, "Now you're acting like you own me..." Is this a reference to Motown's control over the group, the lawsuit over The Jackson 5 name and his musical future? "I have tried to make you change, but you remain the same" could refer to the evening in May 1975 where he tried to reason with him about allowing the group to have creative control.

Also, what is interesting to note is how, at the end of the third chorus, Michael stylistically wails, "turn around," a determined way of saying, "just look over your shoulders honey"[xxxiii] as he did seven years earlier on "I'll Be There" — an ad-lib that Berry Gordy encouraged Michael to make during that song's production. Here one may get the sense that Michael was sarcastically wailing the line as a way of sending a message to Gordy on how he needs to change the authoritarian control he places on his artists and allow them to breathe. At the time of the song's recording, the brothers were still giving depositions for the lawsuit from Motown over their name ownership and breach of contract (signing with another label while under contract with Motown). Writers often send messages to their colleagues through music; perhaps this case was no different. Nevertheless, the brothers still had to prove to the CBS brass that they were capable of complete artistic control for at least another two to three years; in the meantime, they were feeling the glow of advantages that they previously had not experienced in their career. To have two original compositions published and the opportunity to co-produce their original songs for the first time were triumphs in and of themselves.

The Jacksons Mural by artist Felix Maldonado. Depiction of the gatefold photograph of The Jacksons *(1976) Album- Miller Beach Borough, Gary, Indiana*

In October of 1977, the group released their second album for CBS entitled, *Goin' Places*. The album featured two original songs from the brothers and this time they produced both entirely on their own, without any help from Gamble & Huff or the Philly team. Unfortunately, the album went nowhere. There were no hit singles from *Goin' Places*; the self-titled debut album only reached gold status by the Recording Industry Association of America when there were high hopes from the group, the producers, and CBS for platinum sales. The poor cover design featured the quintet in dusty tuxedos, stopping at a country gas station asking three older men for directions as all of them are looking at their maps. Unfortunately, the photo looked more like a still photo from a sketch off the television variety show. (Could this signify the group stopping to Walter Yetkinoff, Ron Alexenburg and Steve Popovitch for direction in their careers at Epic?). As Gamble & Huff were still struggling to find a sound that would fit the group, the music on this album appeared to venture back to the bubblegum sound that they complained about at Motown. During *The Jacksons* album campaign, the group continued their appearances for their prime-time television show where they performed "Enjoy Yourself" and "Show You The Way To Go" to support the record. Michael believed that the television series contributed to the below average sales of the CBS debut and the upcoming LP *Goin' Places*. He complained,

> **You are in people's homes every week and they begin to feel they know you too well. You're doing**

all this silly comedy to canned laughter and your music begins to recede into the background. When you try to get serious again and pick up your career where you left off, you can't because you're overexposed.[xxxiv]

In the spring of '77, the show had plummeted to the bottom of the Nielsen ratings at number 70 for its final presentation on March 9th.

Produced after taping for the series had ceased, *Goin' Places* introduced guitar work from Tito and percussion from Randy. The first composition was an underrated song entitled "Different Kind Of Lady." This production is important in the historical chronicle of the group, because it received a great deal of attention in the dance clubs at the height of the Disco craze. "Different Kind Of Lady" is also significant because it proved to the administration at CBS that the brothers were capable of writing good dance songs and producing potential hit music.

The second song was "Do What You Wanna," a head-bopping, feel good type of song. As producers, the brothers had developed their competency in the studio and were ready to handle advanced responsibilities. Having the skills is one thing; convincing your boss is an entirely different matter altogether. *Goin' Places* debuted at the Billboard 200 Album chart at number 63 and number 11 on the Billboard R & B Album chart. The album sold over 500,000 copies.

The Jacksons, if unbeknownst to them, were beginning to appear "corny," at least to the African American public. Tastes were changing. This was the time when Disco and Funk music were undergoing a metamorphosis in what would eventually become Hip-Hop. Joseph Jackson and his 19-year-old son were growing concerned. More than two years had passed since they had closed their deal with CBS, but they had yet to see the progress they expected. The Jacksons were grateful for some control given, but it was piecemeal. Joseph Jackson felt it was time for a meeting with the brass.

Joe and Michael met with Ron Alexenburg at the CBS headquarters in New York City. The meeting was a special plea from the group to CBS management that the brothers were finally ready to write, arrange and produce an entire album on their own. In the CBS boardroom, where the meeting took place, Joe and Michael explained how unhappy they were at CBS by their handling of the last two albums and how, in Michael's words, "CBS had evidence of what we could do on our own."[xxxv]. If CBS was unwilling for the brothers to control their artistry, then it was time to terminate the contract before more money would be wasted on another low selling project.

Unfortunately, outside of the knowledge of the Jacksons, Walter Yetinkoff already had decided to drop the group from the label. *The Jacksons* (their self-titled CBS debut) and *Goin' Places* were not enough to merit a third album. Bobby Colomby, former drummer of Blood, Sweat and Tears, and head of Epic's West Coast Artist Relations, was under pressure from the company to buy them out. However, as he indicated,

> **I felt so bad for these guys—and I like them, they were so sweet and innocent—I said to myself, My God, if I give these people a hundred thousand dollars to go away, they're going to pay their bills and be out of the business forever.**[xxxvi]

At the meeting, Michael presented his case to have Bobby Taylor co-produce the next album, but Epic wanted Gamble & Huff because of their experience in soul music. Michael remarked,

> **Maybe they were the wrong jockeys or we were the wrong horses for them, because we were letting them down in the sales department through no fault of our own. We told Mr. Alexenburg that Epic had done its best, and it wasn't good enough. We felt we could do better, that our reputation was worth putting on the line.**[xxxvii]

As they left the CBS building, Joe Jackson was optimistic; Michael had learned a lot about the music and entertainment business from watching him. However difficult their personal relationship may have been, Joe and Michael Jackson agreed on one thing: that there should be no animosity between artists and executives. Michael Jackson referred to that pivotal day saying, "Our whole lives had been leading to that single, important confrontation, however civilized and aboveboard it was." xxxviii

The Gamble & Huff experience was a fruitful and beneficial experience for the Jackson Brothers. Some observers have suggested that the boys really did not gain much from their fight with Motown. What they did gain from the experience was the opportunity to co-produce two songs on their first CBS album and to produce two songs independently on their second. The Gamble & Huff period was the final training ground for the brothers before they ventured into the unknown as independent songwriters and producers. Through Gamble & Huff, the brothers learned production techniques and composition dynamics. In his 1988 memoir, Michael recalled what he had learned from the kings of Philly Soul.

> **Just watching Huff play the piano while Gamble sang taught me more about the anatomy of a song than anything else. Kenny Gamble is a master melody man. He made me pay closer attention to the melody because of watching him create. They'd come to us in our hotel and play a whole album's worth of music for us. That's the way we'd be introduced to the songs they had chosen for our album—aside from the two songs we were writing ourselves. It was an amazing thing to be present for.** [xxxix]

This education would serve the nineteen-year-old Michael Jackson and his older brothers an immense benefit toward their future, especially within the framework of their next artistic endeavor.

Chapter Two: Pre-Destiny

The Jacksons' 1978 album known as *Destiny* was not a project that materialized after four months in the recording studio; it was the result of the climatic meeting between CBS executives and Joseph and Michael Jackson. The album also totalized their entire ten years in the recording business. As Michael Jackson once said, their lives had been leading to that single, important confrontation at CBS Headquarters. As recording artists, their entire odyssey led them to this zenith of their artistic craftsmanship. *Destiny*, although it was a "Jacksons" album, centered on Michael's life hurdles as an older teenager. Although the album was credited to have been written and produced by the group, it is conclusive that Michael was the driving force. At the age of 19, Michael felt he needed more artistic satisfaction than what the group had been giving him. Pleased with the opportunities to produce a few songs on the first CBS albums, he was disappointed with the poor sales of *Goin' Places* and, in addition, he hated the television variety show featuring his family, but he was forced to go along with it.

As early as 1975, many felt that Michael would be more noteworthy as a solo artist instead of a front man. Jackson had been a solo artist since 1971, and had released five solo records through Motown, but these works were all under the franchise of the Jackson 5. Jermaine and Jackie Jackson had also released solo material while at Motown, but Michael was the most successful. In 1977, rumors began to circulate that Michael was looking to embark on a new and more permanent solo career that would not be a side project from The Jacksons. Katherine Jackson, Michael's mother, recalled a phone call from a lawyer in 1975:

> **One of the lawyers called me one day and told me to tell the other boys that they better start saving their money 'cause Michael was going his own and Michael was only 17 at the time, he hadn't graduated yet and I told him No! I said you can't do that, and he said why? Because, I said, I know**

> **you said that Michael doesn't need his brothers-[sic] but as for right now, they need him.**[xl]

When it came to important business decisions within the group, Michael was often outvoted. This was done to keep a leverage of power within The Jacksons. His brothers and his father knew that he was the most important member; they walked on eggshells around him for fear that if anything were to upset him too much, he may leave the group. In the late 1970's, Michael once told an associate,

> **They don't listen to me because they're afraid to, I guess I can understand that. They don't want to lose me. They don't want me to have too much power. But it makes me mad.**[xli]

The first act of defiance from Michael was pursuing a film career. In early 1977, Motown Productions, the record label's film subsidiary, acquired the rights to The Wiz, the African American musical rendition of L. Frank Baum's, The Wonderful Wizard of OZ. Rob Cohen, the head of Motown Productions, encouraged Michael to audition for the role of the Scarecrow. Once he won the part, Michael's brothers and father were opposed to him taking the role. This time he stood his ground and went forward with the production. He told Cohen,

> **I have to make this film for personal reasons, there are some things I have to prove. To myself and to others."**xlii

In July of 1977, he and his sister LaToya moved to New York City where they resided in an exclusive apartment in Manhattan's Sutton Place on the Upper East Side for the six-month production period for The Wiz. For the first time in their lives, Michael and LaToya lived outside of their parents' home. Working on a Hollywood film shoot on location was a great experience for Michael, and gave him the taste of the independence he savored. Reportedly, he worked hard during the day and played hard in the evening. He socialized more during this time in his life than he would in his future. He associated with the Kennedys, partied at Studio 54, spent time with Truman Capote and Liza Minnelli, and briefly dated singer Stephanie Mills. The biggest benefit from The Wiz was meeting the figure who would become the greatest force in Michael's professional life in the next decade. The music supervisor of the film and producer of the soundtrack album was none other than Quincy Jones. Through their association, Quincy offered to produce Michael's next solo album that Epic promised as part of the Jacksons' recording deal. These experiences, along with the personal turmoil of adolescence and the Motown/CBS fiasco, contributed to the musical content he would later compose into the album known as *Destiny*.

Principal photography on The Wiz wrapped on December 30, 1977. Michael wanted to return to California to begin work on the solo album he and Quincy Jones talked about that would become *Off The Wall*, but his brothers came first. While Michael was in New York, Bobby Colomby was able to persuade CBS to give the group one more chance at Epic with more creative power. If they failed, the label would drop them and they would have no one to blame but themselves. This agreement was activated upon the contingency that Bobby Colomby and veteran producer Mike Atkinson must be on hand to serve as executive producers.

      Shortly after Epic's decision, the brothers formed their own production company, Peacock Productions; it would be an umbrella to house and keep track of the many projects that they foresaw in their careers as writers, arrangers and producers. They also founded for themselves five individual publishing companies. Siggy Music for Jackie, RatTrap Music Publishing for Tito, Vabritmar Music for Marlon, Mijac Music for Michael and Ranjack Music for Randy. The brothers were now men, taking control of their music and destiny. In January 1978, the band embarked on a short U.S. and European tour.[xliii] In spring of that year, preproduction demo recording began at their Hayvenhurst home studio in Encino, CA. From August to November of that year, the boys, along with Colomby and Atkinson, would spend their time recording at Cherokee Recording, Total Experience, Heiders/Filmways, The Record Plant, and Dawnbreakers Recording Studios, all located in the Los Angeles area.

    Personnel for the new album would include some of the finest names in the music business: guitarist, Michael Sembello, horn arranger, Jerry Hey, renowned string arranger, Clare Fischer, and a 22-year-old, up and coming studio professional who would become a loyal keyboardist to the Jacksons and later a driving force in Michael's solo career, Greg Phillinganes.

    Phillinganes' keyboard techniques would contribute by constructing the Jacksons/Michael Jackson sound which the world would come to know. Another valuable musician would also contribute to their funky rhythmic sound. Percussionist, Paulinho de Costa, was brought in by Bobby Colomby. This was due to Epic's concern that 16-year-old Randy would not be able to handle all the percussion by himself for a major album; however, Michael, later commented that de Costa's artistry was welcomed in the group, said

> **Paulinho brought with him the Brazilian samba tradition of adapting and improvising on primitive and often homemade instruments. When de Costa's sound joined forces with Randy's more conventional approach, we seemed to have the whole world covered.**[xliv]

The Jacksons understood they needed outside musicians to get the best possible sound, but it was extremely important to them that Tito be given ample guitar time on tape, that Randy play a prominent role in percussion with help from big brother Jackie, and that Marlon and Michael contribute on composition, harmony arrangement, and production. Formal studio production commenced in August of 1978, shortly before Michael Jackson's 20th birthday; for the first time, Jackson would be able to express his personal feelings in the musical and lyrical form he had been waiting to do.

Although the brothers would release three more albums, *Destiny* has been called The Jacksons' most exciting album of their body of work; it was certainly their most successful at that time. Without having sales figures of one million since 1975, *Destiny* was a welcomed and much deserved change. Certified platinum with a worldwide sales record of 1.8 million copies[xlv], *Destiny* spawned two hit singles making the group a relevant and predominant force in the music industry at the turn of the 1980's pop music scene. The album peaked at number 11 on the Billboard 200 Album chart and number three on the Billboard R&B album chart. One thing that the Jacksons should be commended for is that there were no so-called "album tracks" on *Destiny*. Unlike their discography at Motown and their previous CBS work, every song on the album could stand alone as a single. For the subsequent promotion of the album, The Jacksons launched a 20-month U.S. and European tour. To bespeak of the conviction in the artistry of Michael Jackson in the timelessness of his composition and production, and at the tender age of 20 years old, *Destiny*, to this day, has sold over 4.2 million copies worldwide.[xlvi]

# Chapter Three: Manifest Destiny: The Agony and the Ecstasy Between the Notes (A Musicological Analysis of the *Destiny* Album)

BLAME IT ON THE BOOGIE

"Blame It On The Boogie" 3:36
Written and Composed by Mick Jackson, David Jackson, and Elmar Krohn
Produced by The Jacksons
Recorded and Mixed by Peter Granet, Don Murray
Horn Arrangement by Jerry Hey
Rhythm Arrangement by Greg Phillanganes
Lead Vocal by Michael Jackson

The origins to this song are traced to Yorkshire, England to a German born songwriter named, coincidentally, Michael Jackson (professionally he would style himself as "Mick"). In 1968, Mick and his brothers formed a soul music band named "Jacko" where he served as lead singer and songwriter. Eight years later, Mick decided to leave the band to pursue a solo career. He had his first hit with the single, "You Turn Me On." Encouraged by this success, Mick and his brother David wanted to write a disco song for Stevie Wonder. The intent was something funky with a feel-good vibe. This was the pinnacle of the disco craze, and Mick and his brothers wanted to follow the trend with a track suited for Wonder's voice. After the composition and recording was completed, Peter Kirsten, founder of Germany's Global Records, saw the potential of the song and brought it to the Midem Music Festival in Cannes, France. At the same time, Bobby Colomby was looking for hit songs for the Jackson brothers and heard this song at the festival. The irony here is that Colomby reported back to Epic executives in the U.S. and claimed that he found a new hit for the group written by an Englishman named, "Michael Jackson." As Michael (Joseph Jackson's son) remembers,

> **Fortunately we got a running start with a song that Bobby Colomby brought us called "Blame It on the Boogie." It was an up-tempo, finger-poppin'-time song that was a good vehicle for the band approach we wanted to cultivate. I had fun slurring the chorus: "Blame It on the Boogie" could be sung in one breath without putting my lips together. We had a little fun with the credits on the inner sleeve of the record; "Blame It on the Boogie" was written by three guys from**

England, including one named Michael Jackson. It was a startling coincidence.[xlvii]

Although Mick Jackson's version was recorded first, it was not formally released prior to the festival. The master tape to Mick Jackson's version was missing and caused a delay at the record pressing plant; strangely, the tape appeared several days later. This delay caused both versions of the song to be released within weeks of each other. Atlantic Records released Mick Jackson's version in the U.S. in August of 1978 while The Jacksons' version, released in October, was their biggest showing on the charts since signing to Epic. The press enjoyed the coincidence of the composer and the singer sharing the same name so much that they initiated a competition called, 'The Battle of the Boogie'. The novelty of having two artists on the charts with the same name and the same song was just too good of an opportunity for the media to pass up. Mick Jackson's version peaked at number 15 on the U.K. chart while The Jacksons' peaked at number eight, and in the U.S., Mick Jackson's peaked at number 61 on the Billboard Hot 100 while The Jacksons' version peaked at number 54. On the U.S. Billboard R & B chart, The Jacksons' version went to number three."[xlviii]

The *Destiny* album opens with "Boogie." It was a wise choice because it was an up-tempo number that would help set the mood of the album and a great introduction to the group's new sound. Writing and production were very important to The Jacksons at this point, and though they opened the album with a cover song, it did not matter. With "Blame It On The Boogie," the song was not only to their liking, it was suited musically. Through their production strategy, they were able to make it (stylistically) a "Jacksons" song.

The brothers wrote seven of the eight songs from the album. "Blame It on the Boogie" indicates that the time of "wandering in the wilderness" with Philadelphia International, in search of their new adult sound, had come to a close. The brothers were showing what they had learned from Gamble & Huff and putting it to use. From drummer Rick Marotta's opening fill to the mix of two bass guitars performed by Nathan Watts and Gary King, the world was experiencing a new adult sound from The Jacksons. "Blame It On The Boogie" was a musical statement indicating that the group could compete with the other hot disco acts of the day in the likes of Heatwave, Sister Sledge, and Shalamar.

Mick Jackson's version is a fine, carefully crafted, pop production driven by a conservative beat and achieving the "feel good vibe" that he was looking for. When listening, one can detect easily how the song was originally meant for Stevie Wonder as it is suited to Wonder's voice and mid-tempo sound. The piano is the dominant instrument on his version working in concert with the drums as the opening fill to the song. Mick Jackson highlights the rhythmic mute guitar providing the funky essence needed for the desired vibe. When The Jacksons' version was released, Mick commented,

> **I got such a rush…I was thrilled because their version was incredible! Our version had 100 percent of our heart and soul in it but The Jacksons' version had the magic 2 percent that made it incredible.** [xlix]

On the *Destiny* version, the romantic aesthetic of the song was completed by the strong, tight harmony vocals sung by the brothers. Michael, for the first time, introduced a new vocal affectation. On the fourth measure of the intro, he introduces "eh-hee-hee-hee." This will become a permanent staple in both the group's work and his future solo career. Michael also plays with some vocal gymnastics, putting pizzazz on some lyrics, particularly in the second verse with the line, "I've seen the lightning leave me."[1] Here, Jackson pours electrifying doses of soulful attitude as he smoothly pulls the line with bass and punches it at "leave me" bringing an ample degree of soul to his pulpit on the pre-written sermon on the powers of music and dance. He does this again on the chorus right before the song's breakdown as he slurs in mock bass tone, again in full soulful attitude: "don't blame it on the good times."[li]

The themes present in the song are entirely representative of Michael's poetics. The joys of dancing are so infectious, they can contribute to the end of a relationship, but here, Mick Jackson is not boasting over the joys of music and dancing; he is complaining over another issue that lies in his philosophy: LOVE; this time, he is not getting enough of it because his baby is always dancing "and it wouldn't be a bad thing, but [he is not getting] loving, and that's no lie." [lii] The tempo is faster on The Jacksons' version; it is more aggressive with a "take no prisoners" approach. A wise selection as the album opener, the fire and assertiveness it carries articulates the aggressive statement on how The Jacksons are taking over their lives and their career, which is:

> **Don't blame it on the sunshine/**
> **Don't blame it on the moonlight/**
> **Don't blame it the good times/**
> **Blame It On The Boogie/**[liii]

Author's Collection

PUSH ME AWAY

"Push Me Away" 4:16
Written and Composed by Tito Jackson, Jackie Jackson, Marlon Jackson, Michael Jackson and Randy Jackson
Produced by The Jacksons
Recorded and Mixed by Peter Granet, Don Murray
String Arrangement by Clare Fisher
Vocal Arrangement by The Jacksons
Horn Arrangement by Jerry Hey
Rhythm Arrangement by Greg Phillanganes
Lead Vocal by Michael Jackson

Presenting "Push Me Away" as the second song, after a strong opener, was a smart choice. In a live performance or on an album's sequence, the second song is usually a number that keeps the momentum of excitement that the opening number had set up for the audience. The opener introduces the thesis of the theme or concept for the album; the second cut is a strong supporter of the thesis. The thesis on *Destiny* is the coming of age of five young men taking charge of their life and career; this is evident in "Push Me Away," as Tito performs his first credited guitar solo. Credited to all the

Jacksons, this is an advanced composition featuring a luxurious string arrangement from Clare Fischer and an ambitious production strategy using the elements and concepts of Phil Spector.

In his book, "The Magic and the Madness," writer J. Randy Taraborrelli commented about "Push Me Away" that,

> **...its orchestral sweep and rapturous melody---seems so carefree and effortless. Yet upon closer inspection, it becomes obvious that Michael's delivery is both tightly measured and precise. He knows exactly how to settle his mind on the heart and story of a song in order to create the proper mood.** [liv]

Ballads have always been an area of strength for Michael Jackson. From "I'll Be There" to "One Day in Your Life" to "Dreamer," Jackson appears at his greatest control when delivering a ballad. "Push Me Away" is a song credited to Tito Jackson/Jackie Jackson/Marlon

Jackson/Michael Jackson/Randy Jackson. While we are unclear as to the exact contributions each member made to the song, it is rational to conclude that Michael's influence is the most dominant, at least lyrically. The element that stands out the most in this song is the symphonic strings. The brothers employed the use of the wall of sound with the string orchestra to carry out the lush mood that they wished to convey.

The "wall of sound" is a technique of studio recording created and introduced to the world by record producer Phil Spector. In the 1960's, Spector developed a tightly layered, reverberated sound that used studio musicians to perform the same parts in unison overdubbed several times, continually stacking the tracks on top of each other while adding arrangements for instruments outside of the traditional rhythm section all the way up to symphony orchestras. The sound became tailor made for AM radio as its sound reproduction sounded nearly pristine for that frequency. While there is no "track stacking" of instruments in the rhythm section, the Wall of Sound in "Push Me Away" is provided by the strings and the complex use of the musical arrangements. The strings are front and center; they are the umbrella. There is the Fender Rhodes keyboard track performed by Greg Phillinganes, an acoustic guitar track that seems to help articulate the strings for the rhythm section throughout the verses while the strings rest.

The electric guitar licks, performed by Michael Sembello, are mixed to the right speaker to complement the acoustic guitar arrangement on the left. The bass (also performed by Sembello) seems to introduce the melody structure for the listener as it also serves a dual function of introducing Michael in his melodic performance. Jackson once referred to the "wall of sound" when talking about his brothers' work. When speaking about the pre-production sessions for the album in 1988, Michael referred to the problems concerning the "wall of sound":

> **We liked the vocal tracks that Philly International always put a premium on, but when the mix**

> **came out, we always seemed to be fighting someone else's wall of sound, all those strings and cymbals. We wanted to sound cleaner and more funky, with a flintier bass and sharper horn parts.**[lv]

Indeed, they acquired the "flintier" bass they wanted in "Blame It On The Boogie." Michael and the brothers were looking to escape the strings in hopes of a cleaner sound during pre-production; there was obviously a change of heart during the creative process. The luscious strings on "Push Me Away" allowed the brothers to achieve the cleaner sound that they had been struggling to achieve.

The song's key is in "C," and according to Rita Steblin's "A History of Key Characteristics in the 18th and Early 19th Centuries," the key of "C" denotes "a characteristic of simplicity, naivety and "children's talk." [lvi] "C" is the one key on the piano keyboard that is located between the two staves of the bass and soprano octaves. Jackson's singing voice is fittingly placed in this area as he was a counter tenor, the top end of the male singing voice order that is the equivalent to the ladies' contralto or mezzo-soprano. The root notes of the song are: G/A/ and C. The key of "G" expresses a tender gratitude for true friendship while the key of "A" denotes a declaration of innocent love (the love a son may have for his father and may wish to. express) and the hope of seeing one's beloved again when parting. Perhaps Jackson is musically reaching out to his father and lyrically expresses this in the song?

In the chorus, Jackson sings,

> **I come running back to you/You push me away, you push/you push me away.**[lvii]

By the end of the song, after he sings this passage, the strings musically realign themselves to run back to the object of their desire, as if Jackson realigns himself to run back to his father, only to be pushed away by the one he wishes to form a stronger bond with.

But what were The Jacksons really trying to tell us in the song, especially Michael? At 19-

years-old, Michael Jackson was tackling many personal issues and coming of age problems that would become the foundation for the tragic events that would plague his later years. Yet, he was searching for a comfort or a support that apparently he was not getting at the time.

There were few instances in Michael's life where he felt a deep closeness to his father. The 1977 limousine ride from the CBS headquarters after the two successfully lobbied for the control of their music is an event that stands to be relevant. The meeting at Black Rock (the nickname for the CBS headquarters, known for its dark granite cladding), was, for all one knows, the last time that the two reportedly saw eye-to-eye on an issue as each party was thinking their own thoughts. Michael and his father had appeared to be of the same accord during what he referred to as a "silent ride."

Joseph Jackson was the first to come to the realization that the public images of his sons needed to change. He was the first to see that marketing the family, as a teen idol unit would close the curtain on a long, fruitful career. Most teen idols have careers that last approximately two to three years before newer stars come to replace them. At 17-years-old, Michael Jackson was observing and absorbing the business deals and complications that Berry Gordy and his father dealt with, involving the storm of leaving Motown, that led them to this place. The quest of *Destiny*, the control of artistic integrity and production, began with Joseph Jackson. He was the first to see it before the rest of the boys could. Michael learned from his father how to run the music business and he also learned from him how not to run it.

One year later there would be a great shift in the father/son dynamic. Michael Jackson would fire his father over irreconcilable differences regarding the navigation of his career.

Perhaps in song, Michael is trying to reach out to his father. Jackson once said:

> **My father has always been something of a mystery to me and he knows it. One of the few things I regret most is never**

being able to have a real closeness with him. He built a shell around himself over the years and, once he stopped talking about our family business, he found it hard to relate to us. We'd all be together and he'd just leave the room. Even today it's hard for him to touch on father and son stuff because he's too embarrassed. When I see that he is, I become embarrassed too.[lviii]

Therefore, the meaning behind "Push Me Away" could not solely be about a young man pleading to his woman to shed the façade, and to be real ("Don't you know /These dreams I wish could be the real you and me I come running back to you, you push me away").[lix] It could also be about a son, reaching out to his father pleading for a relationship, something that Jackson admitted that he did not have with his father due to the shell he (Joe) had placed around himself.

**Live and sigh/crying eyes/
Your touch/your heart/
your warmth lullaby**[lx]

Jackson lives with a void that other people his age do not experience, the absence of a substantial relationship with a same gender parent and the expression of the love and affection that exists between them. Jackson has often talked about the differences between he and his father. He once commented that every time he saw him he would regurgitate. Regardless of his feelings he has also shown that he loved his father because we get the idea that he wants to know more about him...Michael comments that he is a mystery. Michael cannot experience his father's touch, heart, or warm lullaby from a man who insisted that all his children call him by his first name, Joseph. So, in the meantime, Michael uses his imagination to dream of having a close, traditional father son relationship as others his age do.

> **Live to dream/don't it seem**
> **The tears/the pain/**
> **Reality**[lxi]

Is the "reality" the tears and pain that come under living within a dark and dysfunctional disciplined structure? Darkness and dysfunction are mentioned because Michael Jackson on many occasions stated that his father abused him and his siblings often and that not only would the child cry as they were beaten but all the siblings would cry for that child…although the beatings stopped in the household after the family moved to California, the scars remain. The "reality" Jackson may speak of in the song could be portrayed as the distance between a man he may admire on one level, and desire to be closer to. Because the career is the priority and his father manages his career and all they discuss are sales figures, promotional tours, concert dates, and business meetings, it can make one question the quality of the relationship. Naturally, Jackson draws the human nurturing he needs from his mother as many of the Jackson children do.

> **Don't you know/**
> **These dreams I wish could be/**
> **The real you and me/**
> **I come running back to you/**
> **You push me away/you push/**
> **You push me away**[lxii]

Michael was whimsical, imaginative, and a dreamer. It is easy to comprehend that he has dreams of not only having a closer and healthier relationship with his father but he also requests for "the real you and me." He wanted both parties to break down the shell, the shell of business, lawyers, agents, careers, etc. and let them be real with one other without the fear of judgement and criticism. But as Michael comes running back to him, Joseph pushes him away. This was simply who Joseph Jackson is. A family relative spoke on Joseph's father, Samuel, mentioning that

> **[Samuel] loved his family, but he was distant and hard to reach," remembered a relative. "He wasn't a warm person. He rarely showed his family any affection so he was misunderstood. People thought he had no feelings, but he did. He was sensitive but didn't know what to do with his sensitivities. Joseph would take after his father in so many ways.[lxiii]**

Evidently, Michael grew up from this dynamic and matured to be quite a sensitive young man. Such sensitivity fed his art and creativity. Joseph and Katherine Jackson maintained that such discipline was needed to keep their children together in Gary, Indiana, in the midst of gang violence, school violence, and teenage pregnancy, among other ills. Jermaine Jackson once remarked, "there were only three outcomes to life in Gary: The [steel] Mill, prison or death." [lxiv] The Jackson children credit their father today for his style of discipline as an aid of forming who they have become.

And as Michael, later in life, came to forgive his father over their disagreements, he learned to accept Joseph where he was emotionally and for who he is. [1]

---

[1] In a 1979 Soul Train interview with Don Cornelius, Michael spoke about the song saying, "it's about a guy who dreams about what he wants to happen in reality but it's...only a dream which is sad."

96

THINGS I DO FOR YOU

"Things I Do For You" 4:05
Written and Composed by Tito Jackson, Jackie Jackson, Marlon Jackson, Michael Jackson and Randy Jackson
Produced by The Jacksons
Recorded and Mixed by Peter Granet, Don Murray
Vocal Arrangement by The Jacksons
Rhythm Arrangement by Greg Phillanganes
Lead Vocal by Michael Jackson

In 1988, Michael Jackson wrote in his autobiography, Moonwalk, the following passage concerning the state of his life during the period of The Wiz and Destiny.

> **There was a lot of uncertainty and excitement about our future. We were going through a lot of creative and personal changes— our music, the family dynamics, our desires and goals. All of this made me think more seriously about how I was spending my life, especially in relation to other people my age. I had always**

> shouldered a lot of responsibility, but it suddenly seemed that everyone wanted a piece of me. There wasn't that much to go around, and I needed to be responsible to myself. I had to take stock of my life and figure out what people wanted from me and to whom I was going to give wholly. It was a hard thing to do, but I had to learn to be wary of some of the people around me. I always found it very difficult to say no to my family and the other people I loved. I would be asked to do something or take care of something and I would agree, even if I worried that it might be more than I could handle.[lxv]

The personal situation alone becomes the lyrical foundation of this album. The Jacksons' first album of original material under their control serves as a chronicle of the turbulent years of Michael Jackson's life. In the above quote, Jackson discusses taking on more responsibilities than he could handle, his inability to say no---especially to members of his family--- and the stress of being aware of others whose objectives are to con him for their personal gain.

In this instance, Jackson once spoke about a colleague who worked with the group on a tour around this time; of the man, Jackson remarked,

> **This guy ripped us off, but he taught me something. He said, "Listen, all these people work for *you*. You don't work for *them*. You are paying *them*." He kept telling me that. Finally, I began to understand what he meant. It was an entirely new concept for me because at Motown, everything was done for us. Other people made our decisions. I've been mentally scarred by that experience. "You've got to wear this. You've got to do these songs. You are going here. You are going to do this interview and that TV show." When he told me I was in control, I finally woke up. I realized he was right."[lxvi]**

Experiences such as these may have served as the fuel for the following lines,

> **Always wanting something for nothing/**
> **Especially what they don't deserve/**
> **Reaching in my pocket/**
> **I just got to stop it/**
> **Even though they got a lot of nerve**[lxvii]

With control so central to his coming of age, Jackson roars out his concerns to us.

"Things I Do For You" could have been a message to his family on how they rejected his opportunity to work on The Wiz because they feared that he would outgrow the act and leave the group as well as his disgust with participating in the CBS variety show. Once again, family obligations meant sacrificing his personal career pursuits. The vigor in Jackson's voice, as he sings this song about giving in to other people, with the feeling that he is being taken advantage of, subtextually implies there may be the obligation of participating in the production of the *Destiny* album itself. When Jackson returned from New York, he wanted to start work on his solo album with Quincy Jones; instead, he brought his creative energies to this project. Sacrifice for a young 20-year-old man undergoing many growing pains brings on a lot of pressure; Jackson's therapy was to write about it. Songs like "Things I Do For You," "Bless His Soul," and "That's What You Get (For Being Polite)," contain a central theme of the album, a responsibility for one's self. Through this therapy, Jackson exposes his codependency. He gives in to his family, putting his own career needs aside.

> **People all over the world/**
> **are the same everywhere I go/**
> **I give in to this/I give in**
> **to that Every day it bothers**
> **me so**[lxviii]

He tells us that being Michael Jackson is not easy. The weight and the pain of carrying the direction and the survival of an entire group at 19-years-old is beyond overwhelming. He vents to us as he learns that with people in show business and even within his family, he must be leery…

> **Am I in a bad situation/**
> **People taking me to the extreme/**

> **Am I being used/**
> **I just need a clue/**
> **I don't know which way to go**[lxix]

He takes his problems to a doctor or psychologist and finds that the physician is incompetent in treating him, later he tries spiritual counseling in the form of a palm reader only to find that she knew nothing. Five minutes later he starts to understand that the only one who can get him through this personal debacle is himself, for in the end, it is he, no one else but himself.

> **I started screaming, shouting, acting mad/**
> **No one could help me/**
> **But myself/**
> **But I gave everything I had**[lxx]

As previously stated the songwriting was credited to the group, but there is no question that the song was clearly Michael's soapbox to express what was happening in his world. "Things I Do For You" would be a significant number in the performance future of the brothers, as it would become a concert staple for

The Jacksons' *Destiny, Triumph,* and *Victory* tours as well as his first ever solo tour supporting the 1987 album *BAD*; and it is always positioned as the second song in the set. A jaunty, energetic dance number, we notice for the first time an intense Michael Jackson venting to us about his personal situation.

The song begins with a strong cymbal crash from drummer Ricky Lawson quickly followed by Tito Jackson's guitar lick in the key of E.

Ex.1

E: The key of "mournfulness and restlessness": Christian Schubart's *Ideen zu einer Aesthetik der Tonkunst (1806)*

Lawson then helps to create the buildup to the first verse with a four on the floor bass drum pattern that then leads its way into a conga solo by Randy Jackson. The brass section comes in and pushes the song into momentum. The song is in the key of E minor, which, according to musicologist Christian Schubart, evokes the characteristic of mournfulness and restlessness.[lxxi] This is an interesting assessment as Jackson appears to be restless in his vocal performance...an indication of his restlessness regarding his personal matters.

Although early in their careers as songwriters, we can see a style develop. "Things I Do For You" follows a structure that we see years later on *Thriller's* "Billie Jean."

"Things I Do For You" possesses the structure of:

verse/bridge/chorus/verse/bridge/chorus/solo/chorus

The brothers have adjusted to Jermaine Jackson's departure in the bridge. Marlon slurs out his line "five minutes later" in one breath, going up two half-steps in his vocal fried lower register in a part that years earlier would obviously have been sung by Jermaine. This is how the brothers kept alive the Jackson 5 stylings of trading vocals that they had perfected at Motown (example: "ABC," "I Want You Back"), and carried with them up to this point. The horns are crisp, clear and tight, presumably the result of the production work of Bobby Colomby and Mike Atkinson. We hear the strength of the horns in the second part of the bridge where Jackson vents, "I start screaming and shouting and acting mad!" The horns take on a "stomping" passage of two groupings of three eighth notes followed by sixteenth notes to articulate his tantrum.

Jackson's tantrums over his ills are in this case full of soulful flavor that the horns demonstrate. If this song were to be stripped of its production frills of double tracking, electronic instruments and excessive production, and left alone with the foundation of the acoustic piano arrangement focusing on an E/E minor/A/ and D progression, we will find that this song is rooted in the old-time gospel tradition in its structure. The keys of A and D project joy and warlike emotions[lxxii]; these are characteristics often present in gospel music.

"Things I Do For You" is a clear cry for help from a young superstar who is in crisis simply because he is unable to acquire the tools needed for self-preservation. Jackson had begun to set his mind on great goals and aspirations; none of which would come to pass if he could not keep his own preservation intact. Eventually, he would gain control.

SHAKE YOUR BODY (DOWN TO THE GROUND)

"Shake Your Body (Down to the Ground)" 7:59
Written and Composed by Randy Jackson and Michael Jackson
Produced by The Jacksons
Recorded and Mixed by Peter Granet, Don Murray
Vocal Arrangement by The Jacksons
Horn and String Arrangement by Tom Tom[84]
Rhythm Arrangement by Greg Phillanganes
Lead Vocal by Michael Jackson

One day, Colomby showed up at the Studio to find Michael directing keyboardist Greg Phillinganes and drummer Ed Green on the same repetitive funky groove, with no variations, for twenty minutes. This wasn't how Colomby did things. It didn't sound like a song, just a groove, over and over. ("It was a very strong, memorable melody," recalls Phillinganes, who had come up with the original beat while dabbling on drums." It wasn't a groove that rambled on and didn't have anything to connect with.") But Colomby went with it. After the musicians had cut the track, the producer called in Tom Washington, a well-known horn arranger who went by Tom Tom[84], and asked him to create a horn part for a staccato, Earth, Wind & Fire-type contemporary-soul feel. Over that, Michael sang the first line. Colomby considered it okay. Then he sang the second one---a tense, dissonant, subtle counter-melody that fit perfectly. Colomby thought that was genius. The song became an eight-minute jam called "Shake Your Body Down To The Ground)," a shorter remix of which turned into a huge hit.[lxxiii]

Three songs in this musicological study require special attention. These songs demand considerable observation because they are the only songs on the album where not all five brothers share co-composition credit. "Shake Your Body (Down To the Ground)," "All Night Dancin'," and "That's What You Get (For Being Polite)" were co-written by Michael and brother Randy. The two were the youngest brothers of the nine Jackson children and presented themselves as a formidable songwriting partnership. In addition to these three songs, they would later write, "Give It Up," "The Hurt," and "Lovely One," which in 1980, reached number 12 on the Billboard Hot 100 and number one on the dance chart.[lxxiv]

Steven Randall Jackson was born in 1961. When The Jackson 5 was formed, he was only three years old. While waiting somewhat patiently to become a member of the group, he honed his musicianship by mastering piano, percussion and electric string instruments. By 1974, when the group made a historic string of concerts in Las Vegas, Randy had become a part-time member of the group who played the congas. Upon the Motown departure for CBS records, Randy became a full-time member in Jermaine's absence and kept the group at the original number of five. Michael once stated that Randy was the one family member who gained the most from the record label change. Randy's public image in the group is that of the rebel, the youngest and edgiest brother or rather a curt construction of Michael in juxtaposition to Marlon, who can be viewed as a mature version of Michael. This comparison is made because, first, in birth order, Michael is the middle child between Marlon and Randy and public attention is placed on Michael because of his position as the lead performer; second, the nuances and sounds that denote funkiness, hedonism, and the overall "carpe diem" spirit of the production indicate Randy's youthful nature. Transitioning to CBS provided Randy with the opportunity to expand his songwriting and arranging skills, as well as his keyboarding and percussion proficiency. In *Destiny's* musicology Randy acts as the foundation for Michael's driving creative force.

"Shake Your Body (Down To The Ground)" is the second single off of the album. Released on February 10, 1979, nearly a month after the album's publication, the song became a million-dollar seller for the group and gave them their biggest hit since "Dancing Machine." In the several television appearances the group gave in promoting the song, The Jacksons appeared to the public as grown and "funky" and, to the group's realization, Michael and Randy had conceived a major hit single and a song that would become a concert staple. From the beginning, the song was composed solely for the intention of becoming a hit. A simple dance song, whether conscious or unconscious to The Jacksons, balances the serious lyrical nature of the album with a feel-good theme of dance, party and lust:

> **You walk around this town with your head all up in the sky/**
> **and I do know that I want you/**
> **You tease me with your loving to play hard to get/**
> **'cause you do know that I love it.**
>
> **--Randy Jackson, Michael Jackson**[lxxv]

Beginning on a segue from the fade out of "Things I Do For You," the song begins with a controlled cymbal roll followed by a piano introduction. The musical foundation of "Shake Your Body" is a curious three-chord pattern rooted in the key of G.

Ex.2

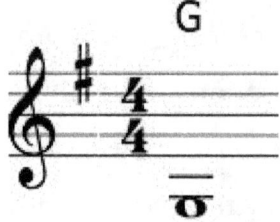

The centerpiece of the *Destiny* album is a groovy, ostinato piano number in the style of James Brown. One can safely assume that the chord progression could have been Randy's conception, considering his proficiency with the instrument, and that his name appears first in the credits. "Shake Your Body" was Randy's groove that Michael helped complete. In a 1979 interview with WBLS' Frankie Crocker, Michael described how the song came about.

> **It was at home and Randy was playing this groove on the piano (he scats the rhythm of the groove) I said what is that? He said aw, its nothing, I said don't say that it is something and I started singing to his playing and it came about.[lxxvi]**

Randy's rebellious spirit is most evident in the bass arrangement. To begin with, no bass guitar is used in the song; it is replaced with a bass synthesizer played by Greg Phillinganes. Phillinganes' performance may have been note for note exactly what Randy wanted as the power source of the opus and the expression of Randy's nature. Greg Phillinganes' performance is so intense, that the sound he produces on the bass synthesizer, the licks, rolls, and the musically sonic comments act as a source of electricity, from the beginning through the middle, and culminates to the end, with an arrogant funky solo.

At the beginning of the arrangement, two measures after the solo piano introduction, Phillinganes gives the band a count of four in quarter notes in the D note followed by a roll before continuing with the rhythmic, syncopated, funky bass pattern.

The bass rhythm is somewhat similar to the rhythm of the bass line in "Things I Do For

You." The walking/shuffling feeling that drives "Things" is also present in "Shake Your Body."

Drummer Ed Green works with Paulinho da Costa to create an intricate percussion line that drives the song along in connection to the bass and provides fuel to the dancer.

The song contains six dance breaks. These breaks serve as a platform for Michael's vocal affectations, especially after the first verse where he grunts on the third and fourth measure of the dance break.

Lyrically and vocally, we see this song as a precursor of both themes and performance style that will later be showcased in Michael's first adult solo album, *Off The Wall*, in the next year, namely, blithe lyrical scenarios articulated by complex vocal gymnastics throughout the song, perfected by a polished production. For example, Jackson's voice is on the tenor octave; on the third verse, Jackson sings the line, "I need to do just something to get closer to your soul"[lxxvii] on a higher register in harmony with a backing vocal (also his voice) and on a lower octave on the line "closer to your soul." It's as if he is emphasizing the point to the girl to whom he is talking. The use of falsetto and tenor voices working together will become a solo trademark style in a future song entitled, "Don't Stop Till' You Get Enough." "Closer to your soul" is the first element of spirituality that we get from Jackson. This lyric is the only element of profundity that we have in this song. Later, the third verse repeats, but with no harmony overdub; again, Jackson is on the higher register. We will see these vocal stylings more in the future in *Thriller* and *Bad*.

The brothers play with new ideas for Michael's voice. We find a great deal of voice doubling reverb effects, starting with the third verse, third chorus, the third dance break with the combo band, the repeated third verse, and at the end of the fourth chorus. At this place, the reverb effect on Michael's voice reaches its zenith as he tells the band to "Take It Over." The structure of the song is as follows:

Introduction

First verse

Chorus

Dance break

Second verse

Chorus

Dance break with strings and horns

Third verse with voice doubling reverb and harmony overdub

Chorus

Horn solo

Band break with Michael's solo voice repeating chorus with a voice doubling reverb

Dance break

Horn solo

Dance break

Third verse repeats with no harmony overdub

Chorus (with reverbed lyric "Take it over")

Horn solo

Chorus (with overdubbed adlibs from Michael and answers from the brothers)

Horn solo

Chorus (abbreviated with only the brothers answering "dance" "and shout!")
Chorus with solo Michael voice

Chorus with handclaps

Dance break

Combo band fade out: horns and strings are cut with handclaps and no effects.

*Bass synthesizer shows off licks with Tito's rhythm guitar driving the piece in conjunction with Phillinganes.

*at the end of the fade out, Phillinganes gives us the final word through the trebly bass lick

    The Jacksons knew that their longevity at Epic would depend on their ability to create hits. Michael and Randy achieved a great deal of confidence upon completion of this song, because they knew that it would be a monster hit. The song was the group's first self-written million-seller hit. Michael called "Shake Your Body" the group's set piece in concert; it is The

Jacksons' anthem and it is usually placed as the show's closing number. Much unlike anything they had done in the past, it is the group's longest number to date, clocking in at seven minutes and fifty-nine seconds, a length that would never have been allowed at Motown. For radio airplay, the song was edited to three minutes and forty-five seconds. Discotheques at the time usually played the album version or the 12" disco single remix clocking in at eight minutes and thirty-seven seconds. This version placed the drum and the rhythm tracks at the center of the song. The 12" remix also featured a new synthesizer-voiced three octave climbing glissando that was not included in the album's mix. [lxxviii]

"Shake Your Body (Down To the Ground)" entered the Billboard R & B Singles Chart on January 27, 1979 where it peaked at number three. On April 21, 1979, the song entered the Billboard Hot 100.[lxxix] On the week of May 19, 1979, "Shake Your Body (Down To The Ground)" peaked at number seven.[lxxx] The song was certified by the Recording Industry Association of America at 2,539,400 copies on June 11, 1979.[lxxxi] It is The Jacksons' biggest selling single to date.[lxxxii]

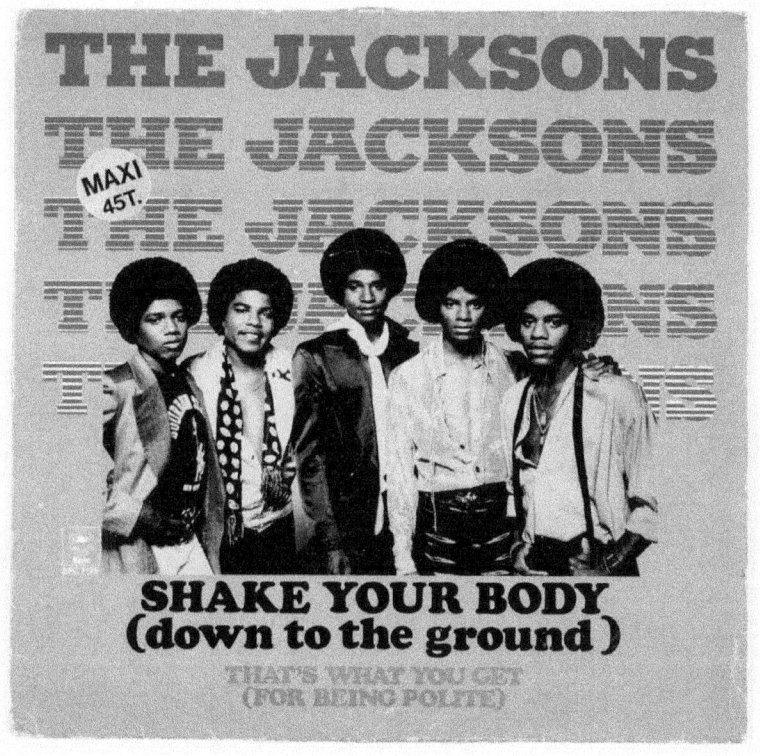

Author's Collection

DESTINY

"Destiny" 4:50

Written and Composed by Tito Jackson, Jackie Jackson, Marlon Jackson, Michael Jackson and Randy Jackson

Produced by The Jacksons

Recorded and Mixed by Peter Granet, Don Murray

Vocal Arrangement by The Jacksons

Rhythm Arrangement by Greg Phillanganes

Horn and String Arrangement by Tom Tom[84]

Lead Vocal by Michael Jackson

What remains to be understood when looking through the Jacksons' musical dynasty that spans 53 years at the time of this writing (approximately more than 60 years if one were to count Joe Jackson's eponymous mid 1950's musical group, The Falcons) is that for their children, Joseph and Katherine Jackson wanted nothing for them but the American dream, the opportunity to rise above poverty by using one's talent and to reach their destiny as successful, world class, history-making recording artists.

Tito, Jackie, Marlon, Michael and Randy may have been cognizant of this as they composed the title song. The song "Destiny" can be interpreted around the theme that the brothers were finally taking full control of their artistic endeavors. The freedom of creative control was the greatest value of their artistic legacy. Destiny, for the Jacksons, meant arriving at the stage of artistic and emotional maturity and truly fulfilling the dreams that their parents desired for them years earlier while living in their two-room house at 2300 Jackson Street in Gary, Indiana. For Michael, destiny may have meant the endeavors that he was yearning to pursue for himself.

The song opens with an acoustic guitar solo, performed as an etude with a slow country feel. This etude perhaps could be an effort to display their musical diversity as sophisticated adult artists or it can be interpreted as a tribute to Katherine Jackson and her musical roots. Born in Barbour County, Alabama, and raised in East Chicago, Indiana, she and her sister Hattie would listen to country-western radio programs for hours on end. Her children would later tell of family sing-alongs with Katherine leading the children with "You Are My Sunshine" and "Cotton Fields," a Southern ditty made popular by Leadbelly. At this point in the album, we truly glimpse the maturity of the brothers. We see their eclectic range in both the songwriting and production necessary for creating music in the Country vein even if the piece happens to be a Pop song with Country elements.

The acoustic guitar etude to "Destiny" is in the key of C Major, a key that denotes an essence of purity.

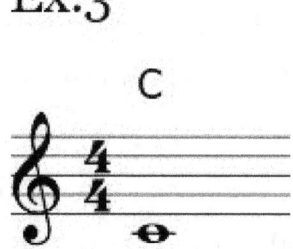

The key of C: The characteristic of purity and innocence: Christian Schubart's Ideen zu einer Aesthetik der Tonkunst (1806)

The quality of the essence of purity is most prevalent in the song, especially in the song's verses. The introduction, through the characteristics of the musical keys described by musicologist Christian Schubert in "Ideen zu eine Aesthetik der Tonkunst (Ideas For An Aesthetic In Tonal Art)," provides feelings of hope, consciousness, contemplation, and complaisance; these elements represent Michael's struggle with his family, especially the obligation to defer to their wishes by often placing his own desires on the back burner.

A drum lick then leads us into a calming country hook well accented by Greg Phillanganes' country style piano, which meshes well with the rhythm guitars of Paul Jackson and Mike Sembello who sustain the introspective feel throughout the verse where the chord progression is also in C. Tito keeps the country feel through his acoustic performance while Sembello confirms the feel by answering Michael's vocals with country licks at the end of each phrase.

The root chords of the chorus are A minor and D minor which respectively denote a tenderness of character and eccentricity. In the second verse, the orchestra makes its appearance with the brothers' harmonies to support Michael. The oboe is the instrument that takes center stage from the orchestra in the second verse. This double reed instrument, with a soprano range, is the one instrument that is the best companion to Jackson's counter tenor in the song. As Michael talks of greeting the stars where there are no stars to see, it is as though his brother's harmonies attest or support his claim.

The second part of the verse. "Destiny," in an inverted sort of way, continues the evolution of Jackson's personal composition style. Earlier, we spoke of a style that consists of:

Verse/Bridge/Verse/Bridge/Chorus, etc.

Here, Jackson does not provide a "bridge" within the verse, but instead gives us a "pre-chorus" that changes direction as he changes thought. When he talks of "If it's the rich life, I don't want it/Happiness ain't always material things[lxxxiii]," the progression lifts us up to a higher level of thinking that confirms to us that we should reach for more and not to settle for what is below average in our circumstances. This takes us to the chorus where Michael cries,

**I want destiny/
It's the place for me.**[lxxxiv]

After the second verse and second chorus, Michael and the band reach the bridge. The song makes a turn from the "cotton fields" to the funky L.A. streets. The country feel loses its momentum as the electric guitars are performing solo licks with the "crunch" distortion effect and as they answer Michael's vocals; we no longer hear Phillanganes' piano as we now hear a Fender Rhodes support the rocking electric guitar licks.

The singing group, who previously paid homage to their Southern country roots have shifted their mood and have transformed to a rollicking, funky R&B band who have found their voice and sing about their "Destiny." The final four chords of the bridge once again express the aspiration of hope, the sustenance of calm within confusion and the presence of complaisance, his willingness to please which happened to be his continued struggle at that time.

    Twelve measures past the bridge, the band and orchestra meld into a singular harmonic mass of warlike intention that builds up the emotional intensity through eight triplet rolls (each one with the extra count of one beat) to a whole note of "A," a key that projects the state of joy and pastoral, rural settings. At last the protagonist returns to the pastoral state within, like a sort of nirvana, or in this case his "destiny," in where he finds inner peace. Later, the band takes it home with the chorus progression of A minor and D minor while the brass makes their presence known with the rhythm combo.

With all that Michael Jackson went through in 1977, he was looking for his destiny. This is no surprise that the young man, whom he was portraying in the song, was himself. But there is a double-edged message in "Destiny." As the lead singer, Jackson metaphorically speaks for the brothers in that, following the painful experience of leaving Motown and trudging through the legal depositions and Jermaine's decision to stay, they have made it through as a family and as artists. For Michael alone, the song is the verbalization of the turmoil he was feeling at this time. During these turbulent years, Jackson often expressed that inside of him, he had so much music that needed to be birthed. Forced to star in projects that were poor artistic decisions, and fighting with his family to expand on his own artistry, Jackson tells of his innermost feelings through the guise of a country boy who dreams of distant places however, he has no desire for the rich life. Michael is a man of all seasons who desires simplicity, a man who vows to search the world until he finds his destiny.

**In this world there's much confusion/
And I've tasted the city life and
it's not for me/
Now I do dream of distant places/
Where? I don't know now, but it's
destiny...**[lxxxv]

When Jackson speaks of "this world" and how "there's much confusion," he could be referring to the real world in which we all live and share an existence, or the world of Jacksonia headed by Papa Joe. Perhaps in this space, there is much confusion over professional matters and confusion over familial matters and internal confusion. Many people in their younger years struggle with who they are going to be or what the future will bring for them. Was it different for Michael Jackson? Yes and no.

No, it was not different for him because there was a prevalent question regarding the growth of Michael Jackson. Was he capable of being a man while secretly longing to be the child he always wanted to be? Many people outside of the public eye deal with this common conundrum. And yes, it was different because let us not forget, he had lost his childhood and yet, he had made his fortune years earlier; his future was cemented as an entertainer with a possible lifetime security that most ordinary people would not experience. However, he was dealing with social ills, loneliness, and an uncertainty over the kind of entertainer he could be as he continued his adult development. As Michael recalled,

> **During this period in my life, I was searching, both consciously and unconsciously. I was feeling some stress and anxiety about what I wanted to do with my life now that I was an adult."**[lxxxvi]

The song provides clues that Jackson desired either to become the biggest star in the world, even at the age of 20, or at least to grow artistically on an individual basis away from his brothers. He collided with confusion. In the nucleus of his world, "the city" could mean show business, or the illicit pleasures of the world. Jackson's spirituality was of prime importance. He was a devout Jehovah's Witness in a profession where there is great temptation (particularly with drugs and sex). "The city" could refer to a possible future being "stuck" as the lead singer of a family group for the rest of his life. Jackson was sometimes paranoid or anxious during the creation of this album because it was gamble for them. He was afraid that if this new sound failed for CBS, there may not be a solo album for him after all. Therefore, Destiny, the album, was extremely important for Michael. Again, Michael stated that "...if the Jacksons couldn't make their new sound work, they could try to turn me into something they could mold for the rest of my life."[lxxxvii] Either way, he had "tasted the city life and it's not for [him]."

In "Destiny," Jackson speaks of escape and flight:

I'm getting away from here

Or

**I wanna get far from here/
or should I up and fly away
so fancy free yeah**[lxxxviii]

Could destiny be flight from the family nest and how it is no different from a bird who comes out of a cage and stretches her wings and flies away?² Jackson comments on the recognition of his own maturity in the second verse and makes a somewhat prophetic statement,

> **Now I'm a <u>man</u> that's for all seasons/**
> **and what the city offers me ain't naturally/I look to greet the stars but there are no stars to see/**
> **I'm gonna search this world until I find my destiny.**[lxxxix]

Michael Jackson was 20-years-old when he wrote those lyrics. One year later, in August of 1979, two events occurred: (1), *Off The Wall*, Jackson's first adult solo album, was released and would eventually make history as the first album ever to yield four top ten singles; (2), Jackson fired his father as his personal manager

---

[2] In 1988, Jackson did fly away from the nest of Hayvenhurst when he purchased Neverland Valley Ranch in Los Olivos, CA. His parents found out that he had moved from the family compound one evening when they watched a television program that reported his purchase of the property. His not telling his parents was an assertion of his independence.

and took control of his own business affairs by hiring Freddy DeMann (who would later become responsible for launching Madonna into superstardom) and Ron Weisner as his personal managers.

Four years later, Michael Jackson, along with these two men, would launch the biggest selling album in the history of recorded sound.

BLESS HIS SOUL

"Bless His Soul" 4:55
Written and Composed by Tito Jackson, Jackie Jackson, Marlon Jackson, Michael Jackson and Randy Jackson
Produced by The Jacksons
Recorded and Mixed by Peter Granet, Don Murray
Vocal Arrangement by The Jacksons
Rhythm Arrangement by Greg Phillanganes
Horn and String Arrangement by Tom Tom[84]
Co-Lead Vocals by Michael Jackson and Jackie Jackson

"Bless His Soul" is one of the most underrated Jacksons' songs in their canon. This song continues the underlying central theme of Michael Jackson's struggles in the late 1970's and how this turbulence served as a stepping-stone for him to realize his true destiny in the 1980's. Jackson continues to open himself up and in a lyrical fashion, this allows us to see the realities of his life as he did in "Things I Do For You" and later in "That's What You Get (For

Being Polite)." The title, "Bless His Soul," refers to Michael's search for spiritual support through this time of great change. Triumph over difficulty is mentioned because the root chords of the song are B & F#. The key of F# denotes victory over a trial or tribulation and Michael's standing his ground to star in "The Wiz" and learning to say no to associates and family are victories in themselves.

"Bless His Soul" begins as if someone is winding up a child's music box. Greg Philliganes performs the melodic music box cadence on a synthesizer in the key of B denoting despair with the next measure in F#. The strings quickly follow in a swirling wind-like entrance into the song. The strings, in their swift blossoming manner, create the picture of the opening of a jack in the box. The "Jack" in the box is Michael and we will come to understand how he fits the character of a "Jack" in a later song.

Following the strings' entrance, the brass section plays a suspended five chord in the key of B.

Ex.4

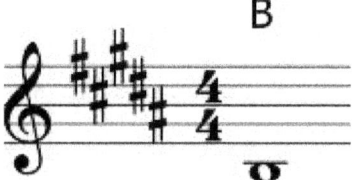

The key of B: The characteristic of despair; every burden of the heart lies in its sphere: Christian Schubart's *Ideen zu einer Aesthetik der Tonkunst (1806)*

This ushers in the lead vocal and the rest of the rhythm section. The structure always carries us back to B major, a key that Christian Schubert wrote,

> **Strongly coloured, announcing wild passions, composed from the most glaring colours. Anger, rage, jealousy, fury, despair and every burden of the heart lies in its sphere.**[24]

Accompanying Jackson's vocals is Tito's muffled rhythm guitar which answers and supports Michael's vocal passages, while Mike

Sembello responds with clean guitar licks in the right speaker. Tito's muffled rhythm guitar line falls in line with Nathan Watts' bass line, which follows the verse progression in an inverted pattern of the Verse passage.

In the second verse, the orchestra plays a greater role; we hear their presence more in the form of brass and pizzicato strings responding to Michael's woes.

> **Sometimes I cry 'cause I'm confused/**
> **Is this a fact of being used/**
> **There is no life for me at all/**
> **'Cause I give myself at beck and call**[xc]

One may receive the idea that the orchestral response to Michael's call may be support for him. The sounds here create the aesthetic representation of angels or cherubs. This idea is not outlandish because Jackson's faith greatly comforted him, mostly because he always knew that, no matter what anyone else's needs were, for him, God came first.

> **I had to take stock of my life and figure out what people wanted from me and to whom I was going to give wholly. It was a hard thing for me to do, but I had to learn to be wary of some of the people around me. God was at the top of my priorities, and my mother and father and brothers and sisters followed.**[xci]

The soprano sounds of the pizzicato, brass and guitar could symbolize the supporting of animals and nature through his "changing times." This insight is relevant because within three years, Jackson does in fact, surround the back lot of his family's Hayvenhurst estate with a personal zoo. The personal changes that the public would see were the result of Jackson's realization that he must place himself and his desires first.

In the previously quoted verse, Jackson speaks of "confusion." As with "Destiny," we indicated that he was dealing with the growing pains of becoming a man. Indeed, this task must have been really difficult for him, as he grew up in a business, even as he matured, he was pressured to maintain his youthful image and now is forced to become a man quicker than he wanted to.

"Destiny" and "Bless His Soul" are songs that deal with this dilemma both musically and lyrically. Through audio-imagery, Michael orchestrates the introduction to "Bless His Soul" as a musical "Jack in the box" to paint the picture that in some instances, he is at odds with the child within.

Nearly ten years later, as he enjoyed the benefits that he reaped. Jackson would be financially able to pursue his inner child through the construction of an amusement park at Neverland Valley Ranch. But for the moment, he was forced to stifle the child within.

In 1963, celebrity counselor and psychic Anthony Norvell wrote a book published by Prentice Hall entitled "The Million Dollar Secret That Lies Hidden Within Your Mind." In the book, Norvell writes that the human being is composed of two entities: the personality and the individual. The individual entity that we all possess is, in reality, perfect and through this entity, we truly manifest the image of the Creator. What is imperfect is the personality. The emotions will get angry, the mind becomes confused, the body becomes sick and these are challenges in life that we must overcome to help us express our true perfection and that, according to Norvell, is our individuality. For a greater understanding of how Jackson conquered this inner turmoil, the author has taken the liberty to divide the lyrics of "Bless His Soul" in three parts: the personality, the individuality and, in addition to the two entities discussed by Norvell, a spiritual entity.

Personality	I try to do what's right for me But no one sees the way I see And then I try to please them so But how far can this pleasing go

Spirituality	Something's soon to come over you You just can't please the world and yourself You gotta start doing what's right for you 'Cause life is being happy yourself
Individuality	Then you should bless his soul It's hard to find A person like you You're one of a kind If I were you, I'd change my mind And start living for me in these changing times"[38]

At the end of the song, Michael, just as he did in "Things I Do For You," comes to a conclusion. After the intense soul searching with his personality and especially his spirituality, realizes that he must strive to become and maintain his true and authentic individual self despite whatever his family may think or feel. He learns that his codependency on his family is dangerous and he must make changes and moreover, he might as well do what is right for him because he can never please everyone.

Individuality	Then you should bless his soul It's hard to find A person like you You're one of a kind People will cry If rain or sun Try to please all And you've pleased none"[xcii]

Jackie Jackson provides co-lead vocals in the song and imaginably, Jackie's performance provides the spirituality that Michael was in contact with during this period in his life. This support is appropriate in that Jackie, being the eldest brother, provides the gentle authority and trust that Michael was seeking at this time. His priority is his spiritual entity and through this song, Michael humbly asks for a blessing.

After the final verse from the "Individuality," the musicians are guided to d.s. al coda or dal segno (where both the listeners and musicians are instructed to return to the introduction), which the second time around does not sound like a child's music box. After the spiritual journey and transformation, the coda, or introduction, is now soft and a more mature and fluid structure of the B F# progression is supported by bass guitar harmonics opposed to the juvenile music box stylings of the beginning. Guitar licks follow and these licks will usher us into a scat-like fade out as the band and orchestra comes in at a slow tempo.

In the fade out, the first portion of the fade out repeats itself then upon its third run, the snare drum picks up driving the tempo forward, which translates triumph over the adversity. The first portion continues into the next portion but instead of ending at B C# B D#, the second portion ends at F# G# F# B denoting a sigh of relief, death (perhaps of the death of immaturity or bad habits), and burdens of the heart. In the end, portion #2 of the fadeout translates triumph of the heavy burdens of the heart and a sigh of relief.

At the beginning of the fade out, we hear Michael solo scatting through the fadeout and, as it repeats each time, we are convinced that his personality has successfully met with his individuality through the guidance of his spirituality.

    Through this guidance Jackson can truly express himself in the way he truly wished (something that he was unable to do at the beginning of the song) to express his true individuality. He will be free to express himself authentically with his original style of tuxedos during the *Off The Wall* period to the conception of the signature "one glove," which was born during the *Triumph* tour and will last throughout his entire career, and later the leather and military style jackets that would characterize the *Thriller* era.

In the context of this writing, Jackson's individuality sings in the bridge,

> **The life you're leading is so *dangerous*/**
> **It's so *dangerous, dangerous*/**
> **all the life you're leading is so *dangerous*/**
> **Doggone *dangerous, dangerous, dangerous*[3].[xciii]**

This is prophecy in the highest regard. Michael was referring to the downward spiral he was currently trapped in by trying to please everyone in his life, possibly to avoid conflict, or the fear of disappointing everyone. He was the lead singer of one of the most popular vocal groups in the country and his family unit looked to him to keep the family enterprise going. The

---

[3] Fifteen years later, success would bring about a dangerous life wherein Jackson would find security in living a careless existence that would plummet him to professional failure, personal economic depression, and the beginning of two false child abuse allegations that would result in a fall from public grace. Interestingly enough, Jackson's problems began during a campaign for an album entitled *Dangerous*.

danger, in his eyes, was continually submitting to his family's needs.

"Bless His Soul" is by no means a quiet storm or a romantic ballad; it is an introspective song that is in one way or another, a form of therapy in dealing with the personal issue of one's maturity and crossing over into adulthood. What makes it so daunting is that the person in crisis, who is documented here, is not an ordinary person---he is a young man who is full of show business experiences and global recognition who in time will possess more burdens to carry than the ones he was wrestling with at that time.

Author's Collection

ALL NIGHT DANCIN'

"All Night Dancin'" 6:09
Written and Composed by Randy Jackson and Michael Jackson
Produced by The Jacksons
Recorded and Mixed by Peter Granet, Don Murray
Vocal Arrangement by The Jacksons
Rhythm Arrangement by Greg Phillanganes
Horn and String Arrangement by Tom Tom[84]
Lead Vocal by Michael Jackson

"All Night Dancin'" is a testament to a joyous and somewhat spiritual practice and yet, a coded synopsis to a personal manifesto concerning the ritual of dance in Jackson's life. As witnessed throughout the years, Jackson's greatest strength, in addition to singing is dancing. Throughout his life, he often proclaimed his love for dancing through music. "Keep On Dancing," "Rock With You," "Everybody," and "Burn This Disco Out" are examples of how dancing plays a critical role in his philosophy of living. In his 1991 poem, "The Dance," Jackson writes:

> **In those moments/**
> **I've felt my spirit soar and become one**
> **with everything that exists.**
> **I become the stars and the moon./**
> **I become the lover and the beloved./**
> **I become the victor and the vanquished./**
> **I become the master and the slave./**
> **I become the singer and the song./**
> **I become the knower and the known./**
> **I keep on dancing/**
> **and then, it is the eternal dance of creation.**
> **The creator and creation merge into one wholeness of joy./**
> **I keep on dancing and dancing/**
> **and dancing, until there is only ....the dance."** [xciv]

Dancing was a staple in Jackson's life away from the workplace of the stage and the sound studio. With the success of *Thriller* in 1983, and with the public more curious than ever on how this young man lived and the nature of his personal rituals, nearly every magazine at that time reported that Jackson spent every Sunday fasting and dancing nonstop to music to the point of exhaustion. This was to feel the freedom or escapism from the drudgery of life and to maintain his thin physical stature. It would not be outlandish to say that, during his lifetime, outside of Jehovah, dancing was his spirituality. He has noted numerous times how James Brown influenced his dancing and stage presence more than any other entertainer. He grew up observing singer/dancers like Jackie Wilson, Sammy Davis, Jr., The Nicholas Brothers, among many others.

By his teen years, Jackson sought to maintain "a dancer's body." Dancers are known to practice anywhere from two to six hours daily, seven days a week; this regimen obviously provides ample opportunities for them to burn hundreds of thousands of calories. Cosmetic appearance as the result of this hard work may have been a benefit for Jackson, but the concern was maintaining a physical frame that would become aesthetically pleasing, as the body creates a fluid illusion brought upon by the art of dance. The old Hollywood dancers of Fred Astaire and Gene Kelly influenced this physiology. Jackson always cited them as some of his influences and in later years, he would refer to them often as more people would become exposed to his dancing talent.

In a 1974 interview with Merv Griffin, fifteen-year-old Michael was asked, "What really [sic] got to you about Fred Astaire?" (Michael had just watched the movie "That's Entertainment.") Michael answered,

Cause he's graceful and he's built for it -he's skinny-I mean-like Gene Kelly, he's just a little wider than Fred Astaire, and Fred Astaire looks smoother. [xcv]

During the *Thriller* and *BAD* periods, Jackson's skinny frame would be criticized and rumors would spread that he suffered from anorexia. The truth was, that there was a reason behind his size, it aided him to perpetuate the fluidity or "smoothness" that he desired from watching Fred Astaire and to incorporate it into his original choreography.

As music became a spiritual quest for the jazz saxophonist, John Coltrane, dancing was no different for Jackson; as explained in his poem, "The Dance," it becomes the closest thing to a religion for him.

Jackson felt this freedom while living in New York for the production of "The Wiz." During the day, he would film the movie and at night, he would frequent Studio 54 and dance all night. Jackson referred to Studio 54 as,

> **Where you come when you want to escape. It's escapism.** [xcvi]

Disco dancing for Michael meant freedom. When Jane Pauley, in 1977, asked why he dances for fun given that he danced for a living, he remarked,

> **You're just being free then. Most of the time its set choreography y'know on stage it's stuff you have to do every night; when you dance here [at Studio**

54] it's free---you dance with whoever you want to. [xcvii]

This conviction is put to music in "All Night Dancin'." This song expresses Michael's feelings about dancing at discotheques, as a young man, in a time where he was able to enjoy himself in such venues. Highlighting the disco experience as he did on "Keep On Dancing" (*The Jacksons,*) and later on "Burn This Disco Out" (*Off The Wall*), "All Night Dancin'," from its conception, is not meant to preach about social ills or cry for universal peace; it is a number meant for "booty shaking" and The Jacksons remind of you this in every chorus.

As we approach the conclusion of the album, The Jacksons give the listener one last chance to groove and shake their booty in dance. The sequencing of "All Night Dancin'," placed as the next to the last song, shows how the brothers were quite aware that they were producing a personally provocative anthology. "All Night Dancin'," breaks the momentum of songs dealing with despair as it pulls the listener up from the emotional doldrums of "Bless His Soul" and makes an effort to bring the listener back to the joy of dance. Written by Randy and Michael, the song is keyboard- based with a gospel feel. The principal chords are G B C Db D F and G. With the song's key in G, Randy and Michael wished to emphasize a state of satisfaction and peace. This peaceful emphasis is hardly the case, when one listens to the band's upbeat tempo, which is driven by the four on the floor bass drum pattern, and accentuated by the Hammond B3 organ. We have the same studio session band backing the group: Nathan Watts on bass, Tito Jackson, Paul Jackson and Mike Sembello on guitar, Greg Philliganes performing all the keyboard instruments, Randy Jackson on congas and Ed Green on drums. At the beginning of the number, we experience an expansion of The Jacksons outside of their comfort zone by allowing a musical warmup between the musicians to be heard on record. We hear the guitarists, Philliganes and Green, warm up on their prospective instruments followed by Ed

Green's audible vocal count of tempo to the musicians in preparation for their performance. Whether this warmup is staged or not, it is clearly outside of the style of The Jacksons, a group who prided themselves on their polished performances, whether on stage or on tape. Listening to the four-second warm up humanizes them and gears the listener up for a joyful experience.

    The foundation of "All Night Dancin'" lies with a keyboard track performing two G notes an octave apart on the upper register of the keyboard. The track is placed in the center of the mix along with the bass and drums. There is distorted rhythm guitar on the left speaker and lead guitar on the right. When the Hammond organ is present, it is positioned in the left speaker at a high volume to give a dominant presence and perhaps to give the listener the illusion that it is placed at the center of the mix. The Hammond organ is the element in the production formula that brings the churchy-gospel sensation. The rhythm guitar on the left is perfectly in tune with the foundational keyboard track in that they are almost indistinguishable.

Nathan East keeps it funky, playing his bass riff with the slap/pop style that accentuates the two and four beat. Tito and Paul Jackson listen to East and feed off each other as their guitar patterns are accentuated in the same places as each player holds their own identities as a rhythm and lead guitarist. Jackson's voice is that of both fury and triumph. During the performance, he displays his James Brown influence through the vocal affectation of "HA!" -- a signature Brown vocal artifice that Jackson accentuates throughout the song. Jackson's cry is of exaltation for the dance. We now feel how he has found joy away from his problems through the ritual of dance.

Jackson talked about escapism with Jane Pauley and in this song, Michael shows us how he can escape from his private angst and familial pressures through "All Night Dancin'." He sings and howls in a fervor that is not present in even "Shake Your Body" or "Blame It On The Boogie." Jackson displays the element of the "preacher" in him and screams with conviction on how it, "ain't nobody's business but mine!" He follows in the Blues tradition with this exalted proclamation; treading on the heels of Bessie Smith and Billie Holiday, Jackson further solidifies and crystallizes the condition of privacy in how African Americans drive their blues away. Whatever one does in dealing with their blues is their business and, in the Blues tradition of Black America, one may choose to share the Blues. In any event, the Blues itself is the force that ignites the creation of the music, the lengths that one may go through to extinguish their blues may be a private matter. Bessie Smith once sang,

> **If I go to church on Sunday/**
> **Then cabaret all day Monday/**
> **Ain't nobody's business if I do.**
>
> **--Porter Grainger & Everett Robbins**[xcviii]

There are two dance breaks in "All Night Dancin'" in which the second one features a hard-rocking distorted guitar solo by Michael

Sembello. This guitar solo is perhaps a penchant for Michael's love for the distorted rock guitar that we will witness years later in "Beat It." After the dance breaks, the sanctification of the ritual rises as it does in the Black gospel church, and the ones who "take it to the church" through the gospel feel of the musical performance are Ed Green and Michael Sembello. Four measures after the second dance break, Phillinganes returns with his organ and prepares us for the buildup; after another four measures, Mike Sembello comes in with his guitar solo and then, in the next phrase, Ed Green provides snare drum fills taking the group to the next level with Michael leading a chorus of "Hey's" that are nothing like his fadeout in "Bless His Soul."

When Michael leads the "Hey" chorus, it is accompanied with a series of handclaps performed in time completing the sanctification of the ritual within the song; The Jacksons are having church and we feel the joy of their sanctity. By the end, the entire band is in sync. They listen to each other, push each other, and bring each participant as well as the dancer, to the greatest ecstasy possible. As we get to the top, the band stops and in solo voice, Michael shouts his mantra of conviction…

Ain't nobody's business but mine![xcix]

We enjoy The Jacksons as a "band" instead of a well-polished singing group where every move in either their stage or audio production is perfected. As they venture into more advanced and somewhat innovative productions in the future, this will be the closest that they will ever get as a garage band.

Therefore, "All Night Dancin'," in its poetics, provides a stepping-stone for the philosophy of dance later to be showcased and highlighted in *Off The Wall* in the coming year. Through all the problems and sorrows this young man carried, we see how he handled them in the only way he knew how, as a performer.

His problems were his own and, to the extent of his passion and principles for "the dance," his private dance or his escapism were nobody's business but his. On stage, we only could witness what he wanted us to see. Otherwise, as he tells us "ain't nobody's business but mine!"

THAT'S WHAT YOU GET (FOR BEING POLITE)

"That's What You Get (For Being Polite)" 4:58
Written and Composed by Randy Jackson and Michael Jackson
Produced by The Jacksons
Recorded and Mixed by Peter Granet, Don Murray
Vocal Arrangement by The Jacksons
Rhythm Arrangement by Greg Phillanganes
Horn and String Arrangement by Tom Tom[84]
Lead Vocal by Michael Jackson

    Traditionally, the closing number of an album summarizes the theme(s) that the artist has laid down throughout the piece either lyrically or musically. *Destiny* follows this practice. A compilation of music containing a balance of enjoyable dance music with songs of introspective profundity, *Destiny* was an album that focused upon the changes of a young man who, whether knowingly or unknowingly, was at the threshold of becoming a force who would join other icons such as Miles Davis, The Beatles, and Elvis in changing the course of popular music. Meanwhile, Jackson followed the therapeutic practices of other artists who have suffered with depression.

Duke Ellington once commented, "I took the energy that it takes to pout, and wrote some blues,"[c] and nineteen-year-old Michael Jackson did just that.

"Push Me Away," "Things I Do For You," "Destiny," and "Bless His Soul" have provided a glimpse of his pain, and now as we approach the album's closing number, Jackson brings us to the nucleus of his pain. The third and final collaboration, between him and his brother Randy on this album, is evident of the strong confidence the two had in each other in creating quality music. As Randy grows and becomes of age, Michael will continue to rely on him. Randy will play percussion on "Don't Stop Till' You Get Enough" and "Workin' Day and Night" in the following year, on Michael's solo album, *Off The Wall*.

"That's What You Get (For Being Polite)" is the most personal song on the album and here Michael lets us know, in a poorly coded (albeit deliberate) fashion, that the song's protagonist is himself. Jackson plays "Jack," obviously a play on his name (or perchance he is the "Jack in the box" in the earlier musical perspective of "Bless His Soul.") Below is a lyrical analysis of "Jack's" plight.

> **Jack still cries day and night/**
> **Jack's not happy with his Life;**[ci]

Contextually, these lyrics arrive to no connection with his father, No direction in career goals.

> **He wants to do this/he wants to do that/**
> **You kind want to be kind but ends up flat for love;**[cii]

These lyrics arrive to "Jack" wanting to start work on his first solo album upon returning from New York but he capitulated to his family as usual.

He tries so hard/to give a lot;[ciii]

Contextually this attributes to Jack giving as much of himself to his family to keep the peace.

He wants to be what he is not;[civ]

Jack wants to be a bigger star than he already is.

So what he's doing for love is so sad;[cv]

A disclosure on his people pleasing.

He wants to be so bad/All the time getting in/things he can't get out; [cvi]

In this context, he speaks of being rebellious, alluding to receiving the bad graces of his father for starring in a movie that did not involve the rest of his family or being involved in an awful television variety show.

Something deep inside of him/eating up the pride of

him/that makes him buy things for the girls; [cvii]

The question arises, why does he have to buy things for girls to fight the source within him that is eating up his pride? Who were the girls? Was it Stephanie Mills? Or later, Tatum O'Neal? Or unknowns?

Jack Still trying to make you happy; [cviii]

Who is he trying to make happy: his family or his fans?

"Jack" may not deliver his treatise of disenchantment entirely to his family; his fans may make it hard sometimes for him to enjoy his privileged position. In December of 1984, Jackson opened up about the treatment he sometimes received from fans:

> **There are those who will come up to you with the worst attitude and will say to you, 'Sit down, sign my baby's paper.' They'll throw it at you. I'll say, 'Do you have a pen?' 'You don't have a pen? Well, go get one.' That's what they'll actually tell me…. I'm amazed by**

some of the people. They think they own you. [cix]

Despite this, "Jack" is still trying to make you happy through his work. He is not proud of how he has handled these social and familial struggles. He chastises himself by saying, "That's What You Get (For Being Polite)."

As to why "Jack" desires to be so "Bad," Jackson once said that he understood his image in the press had been that of a "goody-goody," an element that led the 1980's press into pitching him against Prince as musical rivals. In the 1960's there were The Beatles and The Rolling Stones. In competition, there was a corporate, straight act that parents were comfortable with, and would encourage their children to enjoy versus an act that was anti-establishment, on the cutting edge and pushed the envelope. In the '80's, this kind of pop music rivalry took effect with Jackson and Prince. A conservative artist pitched against a rebellious "rude boy" who ultimately became the target of the Parents Music Resource Center for explicit lyrics (such as Prince). The reality was Jackson was more daring than people realized.

No one is perfect, not even "Jack." His devotion to the Jehovah's Witness faith tradition was played to an extreme in the 80's press but "Jack," (Michael) wanted to be so "Bad" (another prophetic title to a later solo album), was probably wrestling with demons concerning the confines and the restrictions of his faith. How much of a "goody-goody" was Michael after this period (late 1977-early to mid-1978)? Michael shocked America in the April 1985 issue of LIFE Magazine where there was a picture of him sitting on a sofa with Stevie Wonder with a Budweiser in his hand after it was widely reported that he did not drink alcohol. Quincy Jones reported that while Michael did not curse, he had on occasion heard a few curse words come out of him.

As he later rose to power, Michael becomes more sexually suggestive through choreography in his music videos and curses throughout his 1995 album *HIStory*. In his last interview in 2007, Jackson confessed to Ebony magazine's Harriette Cole about his "bad" mouth, "I say a few swear words now — but especially then, [referring to the late 70's-early 80's] you couldn't get me to swear[cx]." He felt the desire to come out of his skin, to become "bad." Jackson spoke about "That's What You Get" in 1988:

> **"That's What You Get for Being Polite" was my way of letting on that I knew I wasn't living in an ivory tower and that I had insecurities and doubts just as all older teenagers do. I was worried about the world and all it had to offer could be passing me by even as I tried to get on top of my field.[cxi]**

The desire to succeed was burning in his late teens. "That's What You Get (For Being Polite)" meshes professional concerns, personal issues, and familial worries; its place in the album's sequencing is appropriate.

The song begins with a G major 9 chord progression, starting with G major 9 performed on an acoustic piano. This chord plays in sort of a jogging rhythm for six beats, before it changes to a B minor for three beats and the measure is closed, before it changes to a D major with E in the bass for two beats to a D Major with an A in the bass to a D Major 6, where it resolves to D Major 7. The orchestra comes in, helping to create the moods of fear, futility, and depression, which brings us through the introduction to the main hook of the song with the song's major keys in D and E minor.

E minor: The key of "grief, mournfulness and restlessness": Hermann von Helmholtz's Tonempfindungen (1863)

E minor is an appropriate key for this song. In Hermann von Helmholtz's classical book about the physics of music theory, Tonempfindungen, E minor is the key that projects grief, mournfulness and restlessness[cxii], and there is no question of "Jack's" restless state.

Randy's congas are present and driving the beat throughout the verses with dominion over Ed Green's drumming. Randy's percussion forms a neat and tight bond with Nathan East's bass. The three players have truly formed the real meaning of a rhythm section. The three guitars work in alignment with Phillinganes' piano; along with the weeping synthesizer solo in the alto octave, also performed by Phillinganes. A wise production choice, the synthesizer solo seems to articulate the pain inside "Jack" and confirms instrumentally how "Jack" cries day and night.

Jackson once said,

> **I like to take sounds and put [sic] them on the microscope and talk about how [sic] we can manipulate the character of it (sound)[cxiii]."**

Indeed, these artistic techniques serve as the precursor for the adult solo sound of Michael Jackson. He receives full support from his brothers here; we hear the rest of his brothers harmonize with him on the chorus of "Jack Still," although Michael is, with no surprise, the more dominant voice in the backing choral mix. Tito takes the center stage from the rest of the guitarists, as he is featured through the filler leads in the song during the fade out at the song. He reaches the forte dynamic on every accented beat in 2 and 4 during the fadeout. Tito's work enhances Paul Jackson's and Michael Sembello's rhythm work in the mix. The guitar answers to Michael's cries in the chorus of "Jack Still" as Michael slurs, "trying to make you happy!" Each time Michael and his brothers intimate "Jack Still," the guitar responds with the first three notes of a D major scale played over a B minor chord so the key of the guitar riff is in D.

The guitar agrees with the cry, the angst of what he feels inside, and articulates to us what that pain is. The guitar creates an affirmative response of its own, responding to Jack's cry. On the 109th measure, during the choral fade out, after Michael screams, "don't you know/he cries!" The horns blast a strong responsive punch in the key of B minor. According to French Baroque composer Marc-Antoine Charpentier from his manuscript, Rules of Composition, the B minor key confirms the state of solitaire and melancholia. [cxiv]

Artistically, "That's What You Get" is a song that could be billed as "The Jacksons featuring Michael Jackson." In addition to maintaining the connection with the rest of the songs on the album (in terms of their extreme personal nature and the therapeutic practice of their composition), the themes in "That's What You Get" are given to us at such an intensity; due to the willful autobiographical message in the lyrics, we see the birth of the adult solo artist of Michael Jackson. Later, group efforts by the brothers will have songs that will clearly be considered solo Michael Jackson songs. The 1980 album *Triumph* will see "This Place Hotel (Heartbreak Hotel)" become one of two Jacksons' songs to be performed on his first ever solo tour in 1987 (with the other being "Things I Do For You"), with the exception of the Motown Jackson 5 medley. The 1984 album *Victory* will see the duet between Jackson and Mick Jagger with the top ten hit "State of Shock" and the acoustic centerpiece "Be Not Always." In all cases, the songs were written and produced entirely by Michael.

If *Destiny* is the journey of finding one's self, one will find in the later works of *Off The Wall* and The Jacksons' *Triumph* that Jackson is maturing, putting himself first and spreading himself more to others on his own terms rather than the terms of his family and other authority figures. He will become involved in projects that are more independent by producing Diana Ross' *Muscles* in 1981, and in the same year, collaborating with Paul McCartney with two songs, "The Man" and "Say Say Say." Perhaps Jackson arrived at his manhood with the production and the release of *Thriller*, a true independent project where he called the shots and expressed himself as an individual.

The Jacksons fulfilled their destiny as musicians, writers, arrangers and producers, but the one brother for whom this period meant the most was Michael. As he told Rob Cohen, the head of Motown Productions, shortly after he was cast in "The Wiz,"

> **I have to make this film for personal reasons; there are some things I have to prove. To myself and to others.** [cxv]

Perchance this motivation may have been the case for *Destiny*. Conceivably, Jackson may have been reluctant to start work on this album, and perhaps after his work on *Destiny* progressed he saw the project as the therapy he needed to fight his insecurities. *Destiny* is step one in the training ground for the future adult mega superstar with *Off The Wall*, *Triumph*, *The Jacksons LIVE*, and *Thriller* to follow. For all involved, especially for the lead man, destiny was fulfilled.

Chapter Four: This Is It: The Musicological Correlation between "This Is It" and "Bless His Soul"

THIS IS IT

"This Is It" 3:37 (album version), 4:55 (orchestra version)
Written and Composed by Michael Jackson and Paul Anka
Produced by Michael Jackson, John McClain, Meryn Warren
Recorded by Jon Nettlesbey
Assistant Engineering by Wesley Seidman
Mixed by Allen Sides
Vocal & Rhythm Arrangements by Mervyn Warren
String Arrangement by Clare Fischer
Bass Vocals by Alvin Chea
Background Vocals by The Jacksons
Lead Vocal by Michael Jackson

After a lifelong career as one of the world's most popular entertainers; the best-selling music artist of all time, globally titled the "King of Pop"; revolutionizing the music business by becoming a leader in the 1980's music video revolution; and making countless contributions to world culture in the areas of music, dance, and fashion; Michael Joseph Jackson died of cardiac arrest at his Holmby Hills, California, home on June 25, 2009. He ended a 40-year odyssey of life as a public and revolutionary figure in recorded music. What Jackson yearned and hoped for in his life that he did express on *Destiny,* did occur, but it did not last. In the span of 30 years, Jackson had experienced the greatest rise of fame, fortune, and success of any man in the common era; he also experienced public shame, gratuitous financial debt, and a traumatic fall from grace.

At the time of his death, Jackson was in rehearsals for what would become his final world tour. He hoped this tour would put him back into the public spotlight from two false child abuse allegations, one of which resulted in a public trial that resulted in media "circus-like" publicity, bizarre reports of his lifestyle, and two failed marriages. On March 5, 2009, Jackson called a press conference at London's 02 arena, inviting both fans and the world media, to announce that he would perform the greatest hits from his career, for what he would emphasize would be the last time. Jackson emphatically stated that *this was it*, that this was really his final tour. As Jackson had these words used as a promotional device since 1981's *Triumph* tour, to publicize every tour as the last, this time he meant it. "When I say this is it, it really means this is it."[50]

He was aging; he had to be cognizant on the state of his body as a dancer, and he wanted this opportunity to perform for his three children who never got to see him perform live. Without a new album in eight years, with a myriad of personal problems and with the changing musical taste of the public, not to mention the changes in the technology as to how the public purchased music, Jackson was indeed serious.

Eerily, his announcement was prophetic. Much of the *This is It* period seemed very coincidental as if, on some subconscious level, he was already aware of the time he had before him.

In the late spring of 2009, dancers were auditioned and rehearsals began at the Staples

Center in Los Angeles, California. Three weeks before opening (scheduled for July 13, 2009), Jackson passed away. An announcement shared, "AEG Live, the concert promoters of the tour, offered either full refunds to all ticket holders or a special souvenir ticket designed by the entertainer." [51]

Following Jackson's death, AEG announced that they had over "100 hours of footage of preparations and rehearsals for the shows."[52] Columbia Pictures and AEG Live reached a deal through the Los Angeles Superior Court for Columbia to purchase and distribute rehearsal footage of Jackson's final rehearsals for a film to be entitled *Michael Jackson's This Is It*,[53] directed by Kenny Ortega, who was also the director of the live concert. The film would be compiled from footage that was shot solely for production purposes. The film was released on October 28, 2009.

Accompanying the film was a soundtrack album: a compilation of the original studio versions of the songs performed in the rehearsals. Released internationally on October

26, 2009, and to North America on October 27th, 2009, the two-disc album featured Jackson's biggest hits throughout his solo career arranged in the same sequence as they would have appeared in the final concert. The album ends with the title track and previously unreleased song, "This Is It."

The song has a long and somewhat complicated history. Its origins go back to 1983, as a composition jointly composed by Paul Anka and Michael Jackson under the original title, "I Never Heard." Anka originally intended the song to be included on his duets album, *Walk A Fine Line* (released in 1983). The demo for the song was recorded at Anka's Carmel, California recording studio in 1983.[54] Shortly thereafter, Anka angrily accused Jackson of stealing the master tapes from his studio. Jackson returned the tapes to Anka, but because Jackson was the song's co-writer, Anka insisted that he make a copy of the demo for himself. In 1990, Anka allowed the Puerto Rican recording artist Sa-Fire to record "I Never Heard" for her album *I Wasn't Born Yesterday*, which was released in 1991.

Reportedly, Jackson planned to release his representation of the song, entitled, "This Is It", to coincide with the launch of his tour. With his untimely death bringing all attention toward the aborted project along with the formation of the artist's estate, the plans for the single were temporarily shelved.

In the late summer of 2009, Jackson's copy of the demo was found in a box of previous unreleased material. SONY and Jackson's estate decided to release the song as part of the *This Is It* package for the fall. Without SONY Music Entertainment (Jackson's label at that time) knowing anything about the history and the composers of the song, they released it to radio with the full credit going to Jackson. Once the song was released, Anka told the *New York Times*, that "This Is It" was "exactly the same song" as "I Never Heard", only the titles were different.[55] While Anka was planning to take legal action against Jackson's estate, Jackson's estate readily acknowledged Anka as the co-writer of the song and agreed to distribute 50% of the songwriter royalties to him. Anka later commented that the estate "did the right thing," and that he felt that he did not think "that anybody tried to do the wrong thing "and it was "an honest mistake."

> **[It was] an honest mistake. I want to clear the record. I've spoken to the estate, they understood that this have been a mistake - an honest mistake; they have clarified the issue; we are moving forward in a very - very positive manner; I've heard the record, they made some major adjustments on the production I started with Michael in my studio in '83.**
>
> **I like the way that it sounds, I like that now that we all understand that this mistake will now be turned into a positive - and whatever I have to do to help them in promotion, because they have been very forthright, they're giving me exactly what is fair and deserved in terms of my ownership of this track and the song and we are moving forward. I really must applaud McClain and Branca and all those involved, who came forth, and realized right away that there was a wrong here and they made it very right and I don't want anymore negative on Michael's grave-may he rest in peace.** [cxvi][cxvii]

Rob Stringer, the chairman of the Epic Label Group, stated that he did not know anything about the original tape.

"This Is It" received critical acclaim from most critics. For the first time in years, Jackson received positive notice for his work. The song was his first Adult Contemporary hit since 1996's "You Are Not Alone." "This Is It" peaked at number five in Japan and number 18 in the U.S. in both the Hot Adult Contemporary and R & B charts. Production included harmonies provided by his brothers, making it the first time in 39 years, since 1970's "I'll Be There," that The Jacksons, then credited as "The Jackson 5", charted together on the Adult Contemporary chart.

Michael's destiny was fulfilled both during his life and posthumously. After an incredible career with an eternal legacy, Jackson made a final showing on the charts with his brothers performing vocal harmonies in the song. The song is a mid-tempo keyboard ballad bearing a striking similarity to "Bless His Soul", especially in the bridge. As the liberty was taken in this writing to inspect "Bless His Soul" in the three components of the personality, individuality, and spirituality, it could be concluded that in 1983, Jackson had found and achieved what his *spirituality* advised him to do in "Bless His Soul". Lyrically, he is talking about falling in love; subtextually, for all one knows, it could be about finding the love and bliss within the young man who was searching for his *Destiny* a few short years earlier.

> **"This is it/**
> **I can feel/**
> **I'm the light of the world**
> **This is real"** [cxviii]

The song's key is in Bb major, a complete turnaround from the melancholic strains of despair in "Bless His Soul" which was in B natural. The opening lower octave notes are known as a "Bb pedal tone." A pedal tone is when the notes played, usually bass notes, remain the same in one part of the harmonic series while the chords, through a successive harmony part, make their usual chord changes.

In the piece arrangement of "This Is It," the Bb pedal tone plays from the left hand while the chords played on the top go from Bb major to Eb major, in the right hand. From "Bless His Soul," which was in B natural and expressed a condition of despair and heavy burden of the heart, to "This Is It" whose key in Bb major, is a key of great positivity and contentment.

Ex. 6

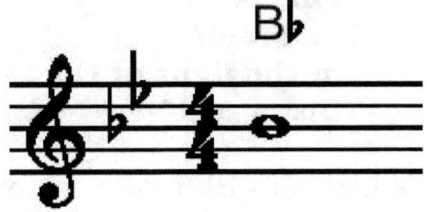

Our protagonist has traveled a half step to a new level of positive consciousness. "This Is It" presents a personal circumstance expressing cheerful love, clear conscience, hope, and aspiration for a better world. There is hope for a better world for himself despite all that he had gone through in the past twenty years.

"This Is It" and "Bless His Soul" offer themselves to comparison due to the similarity of musical strains within their bridge components. In the purposes of this writing, where we placed Jackie Jackson in the context of portraying the spiritual force who counsels Michael to do what's right for him in the bridge of "Bless His Soul", we see the return of such ethereality also present in the bridge of "This Is It". The pre-bridge chords of the song are in Ab to Bb, where we are warned of the premonition of imminent death or transition from human form to eternal status. The complete bridge takes us from Eb/Bb to F/Bb. He had now arrived at the peace of mind that he had been longing for; the search for love, self-love, and devotion is now over as he has found all these things and has arrived at a state of bliss.

Eb is also characteristic of the intimate conversation with God, an experience often noted by many prior to one's transition. We see the connection between "This Is It" and "Bless His Soul" because, while the bridge of "This Is It" is in Eb/Bb to F/Bb, the bridge of "Bless His Soul" contains E natural and B natural.

Where the bridge portions of both songs are concerned, Jackson has matured from not feeling completely whole as a man, and lamenting the dark burden he carried in his heart; to now experiencing the intimate conversation with God, and holding on the hope for a better world which he may be preparing himself for leaving.

Lyrically, the wholeness, fulfillment of control, and maturity are celebrated in the guise of falling in love. Jackson is telling us that "this is it;" that what he had been waiting for, the fulfillment of his destiny, has arrived. Very telling that the song was written in 1983, when Jackson finally appeared to be at peace with himself after releasing *Thriller*, and feeling as if he has finally come into his own as a grown man who does not have answer to anyone, something he had trouble with from his late teens to the age of 24. From the introduction of "Bless His Soul", a number that musically resembled that of a jack-in-the-box toy, Jackson reached the burning sands of his maturity here in his last adult contemporary hit.

The King of Pop Michael Jackson Commemorative Coin - Author's Collection

EPILOGUE: FULFILLED DESTINY

Ebony Magazine ad for Destiny *Album - Author's Collection*

On December 17, 1978, CBS/Epic Records released the *Destiny* album to an overwhelmingly positive public reception. Eight weeks earlier, "Blame It On The Boogie" was released as the lead single. The song brought The Jacksons back to the Billboard Hot 100 chart, after several poorly performed singles since their transition to CBS from Motown. "Shake Your Body (Down To The Ground)," released on February 10, 1979, confirmed for the public the group's adulthood and returned them to the top ten with the biggest selling single of their discography. The road had been long and hard for the Jackson Brothers. They had left Motown over lack of creative control, and they had no major hit singles. They had signed with one of the most powerful record companies in the world who had doubts of them achieving career success, let alone their competency in the execution and leadership in the production of their work; they had spent two of those three years convincing the powers in charge that they were competent writers and producers. Finally, as teenagers, they had participated as co-defendants by giving depositions in a corporate lawsuit for leaving Motown Records before their contract expired. Furthermore, while all of this upheaval was happening, they were forced to star in a substandard television variety show, which had brought misery to the show's featured performer.

Moreover, the C.E.O. at CBS, unbeknownst to the brothers, had plans of terminating them from the label.

Indeed, these challenges appeared to lead them through the journey to *Destiny*. Michael Jackson took all those experiences, positive and negative, and along with his brothers, poured them into a creative cauldron and stirred the contents, crystalizing them, and created this superior production. Making the transition into adulthood, in Jackson's case, it was an ordeal that the average teenager could never bear because Jackson was a public figure. Joe Jackson once said,

> **When you're in the public eye, your life is in the public domain. People read about you, they write about you. They draw their own conclusions.** [cxix]

Both in the industry and in the public, the conclusion had been that The Jacksons were all but dead; the truth is they were just getting started. If Bobby Colomby had not convinced

Walter Yetnikoff to take a chance on them, The Jacksons, along with several other adolescent groups of their time, may have been forgotten. All they needed was a chance to prove themselves. *Destiny* was the manifest vehicle to present such excellence. We should not remember the project solely as the venue in which the brothers produced and wrote their own material. While their authentic work is significant, we must also see the project as a diary and a prophecy of the struggles of Michael Jackson.

Destiny re-established the brothers as a top-selling group in the music industry. The album sold four million copies worldwide during its campaign; it was The Jacksons' masterpiece.[cxx] Everything that they had ever worked for since living at 2300 Jackson Street in Gary, Indiana, led them to this apex. In the inside jacket of the album, we see the Jeffrey Scales photograph of the five brothers proudly posing behind the recording console at the Los Angeles Record Plant as mature men.

The Jacksons at the recording console - Author's Collection

The front album cover, designed and painted by Gary Meyer, shows the brothers on top of a giant stone edifice, carved with the word DESTINY. The stone edifice is resting in the middle of a stormy sea. Behind the edifice, we see the thunderstorm, dark clouds, lightning and a tornado, all of which are symbolic of the pain of leaving Motown, enduring the arguments, weathering the lawsuits, and burdened with the doubts from alleged friends and unrelenting enemies.

Destiny Album Cover - Author's Collection

On the back cover, we see the clouds parting, the white mountains in the background, a Peacock sits upon a chrome pedestal, resting in the calmness of the waters; spreading its tail in full color and glory. These images symbolize success in their craftsmanship and their coming of age.

The image of the peacock is the beginning of the recurring motif of the Jacksons up until 1982. The Peacock, largely Michael's brainchild, is a symbol of the group's philosophical poetics on how they use their art as a tool of promoting love and peace. These themes of love, peace and human harmony come from their time working with Gamble & Huff. As Geoff Brown writes in "Michael Jackson: A Life In Music":

> **...in its balance [the musical themes] between dance floor, love interest, and concern for the moral and physical future of mankind and the planet...[it] set the pattern for the first phase of the rest of their lives.**[cxxi]

And to the thought of themes and their connection to artistic maturity, music journalist Kit O'Toole states "[that] already hallmarks of Gamble & Huff productions, those themes [dance floor, the moral and physical failure of mankind] would reappear on future Jacksons' albums such as *Destiny* and *Triumph*." cxxii Underneath the song listing, on the back cover there is a note from Michael and Jackie Jackson which reads:

> **Through the ages, the peacock has been honored and praised for its attractive, illustrious beauty. Of all the bird family, the peacock is the only bird that integrates all colors into one, and displays this radiance of fire only when in love.**
>
> **We, like the peacock, try to integrate all races into one through the love of music.** cxxiii

In 1980, Jackson told music historian John Pidgeon,

> **You hear us talk about the peacock a lot because the peacock is the only bird of all the bird family that integrates every color into one. That's our main goal in music. When you go to our concerts and you see every race out there and they're all waving**

hands and they're holding hands and they're smiling and dancing. All colors. That's what's great. That's what keeps me going. cxxiv

Destiny Tour Programme - Author's Collection

On the edifice, three of the brothers, Tito, Marlon, and Randy are dressed in white shirts and pine green chino-like pants. Jackie shows his individuality and perhaps his seniority as the eldest brother by breaking the uniformity, wearing a red shirt. Michael is shown standing on the right, wearing white but with a peach colored scarf and a red vest and, breaking the pattern of his brothers; he is wearing white cargo pants. Even in the cover painting, Michael has declared his individuality, by going against what was expected of him; he placed great importance on the sculpting of his personal identity and the exploration of what was authentically his own.

In this era, of the *Destiny/Off The Wall* period (1978-1979), Michael Jackson was obsessed with his vision of becoming the biggest star in the world. LaToya Jackson once stated that in their Encino, California home, Michael wrote and pasted notes all over his bedroom affirming himself to become the greatest entertainer in the world (visual affirmation notes are a form of neuro self-programming when the information being fed into the unconscious mind, starts to support the conscious mind in order to achieve the manifestation of a personal goal.)

On January 22, 1979, The Jacksons embarked on the *Destiny* tour that supported the album. The tour spanned four legs, playing in Europe, Africa and North America with 83 concerts in the United States alone. On the road for 21 months, Michael was riding high, living and breathing his destiny. He also was able in the greatest way, to achieve this serendipity by recording and releasing the solo album he yearned to work on after leaving "The Wiz."

Off The Wall, produced by Quincy Jones, was released on August 10, 1979. The public fanfare was so great that The Jacksons had to revamp the *Destiny* stage show not only by including songs from *Off The Wall*, but also in costuming and set design. Changes were also made in promoting the show and reconsidering size of the performance venues in order to hold more fans. The Jacksons had to perform in larger arenas because *Off The Wall* added a new audience to the already loyal Jackson 5 fan base. The success of *Off The Wall* brought The Jacksons to superstar status in the recording industry as they, along with Earth, Wind, and

Fire, became one of the first black "arena rock" acts of the late 1970's.

Destiny Tour Pin - Author's Collection

While on this tour, Michael was thinking about what lay ahead of him and thought seriously about who and what he wanted to become. He wrote a vision statement for himself:

> **MJ will be my new name. No more Michael Jackson, I want a whole new character, a whole new look, I should be a totally different person. People should never think of me as the kid who**

> sang *ABC, I Want You Back*. I should be a new incredible actor, singer, dancer that will shock the world. I will do no interviews I will be magic. I will be perfectionist, a researcher, a trainer, a master. I will be better than every great actor roped in one. I must have the most incredible training system to dig and dig and dig until I find.
>
> I will study and look back on the whole world of entertainment and perfect it, take it steps further from where the greatest left off.[53]
>
> --Vision statement of Michael Jackson Written on the Destiny Tour November 6, 1979[cxxv]

If *Destiny* was his cry for help, then, by the end of the project, he had acquired the understanding, the will and the strategy to become his own man. *Off The Wall* was his "Declaration of Independence" and the vision statement of November 6, 1979, was his manifesto. Michael Jackson, MJ, "The Man" was born.

As the Canadian journalist Jason King put it, "He [was] coming out as an autonomous figure separate from his father or separate from his brothers and really establishing himself as a solo act."[cxxvi] Jackson was not to be just any solo act. His vision statement propelled him more on the night of February 27, 1980 at the 22nd Annual Grammy Awards. *Off The Wall*, his most successful solo album at that time, was nominated for two awards (Best R&B vocal performance Male and Best Disco Recording); he only won Best R&B vocal performance for "Don't Stop 'Till You Get Enough." Disappointed and feeling he had been robbed, he told his mother, "Next year they gonna have to give it to me." [cxxvii]

By working day and night, he became a man of many achievements; the first recording artist in history to spawn four top ten singles from a solo album, the first recording artist to win eight American Music Awards in one night and the first recording artist in history to win seven Grammy awards in one night. Awarded 38 times by the Guinness Book of World Records (and to this date (2017) he is still the number one recording artist in the world). In 1993, he upheld the most lucrative recording contract in history with SONY Music and even today in death, he holds the most lucrative posthumous recording contract in history. There are more awards and accomplishments that are too long to list here.

But along with the glory, came the heartache. The price of making it to the top resulted in the end of personal freedom: harassment by the paparazzi, enforced seclusion, speculation over sexual identity, questions about personal lifestyle, and criticism over ethnic identity and ethnic pride, and sadly, the damning criminal accusations, regardless of the multitude of proof of his innocence, these all continue to soil his reputation after his passing.

After spending seven years studying Jackson, I am truly convinced that, if one really needs the answers to any questions over his enigmatic life, eccentricities, and the dark agony of the trials and tribulations, one merely should look within the music. The answers are there. Through his art, Michael Jackson tells us that his development was not arrested and although he related to Peter Pan and felt he was Peter Pan in his heart, the truth was, unlike the character of Pan, Jackson did grow up and became a mature man; and in maturity, he teaches us that it is still important (for all of us) to keep the inner child inside alive.

This entire legacy and musical dynasty was birthed from a dream. From a young man in Arkansas who desired to go west to find his destiny, wealth, and power; with his loving wife, they together harmonized Christmas carols in front of a fireplace in East Chicago, Indiana;

each expressing their aspirations and hopes for the future.

The destiny, wealth, and power of The Jacksons came from the strength and determination of a family descended from Alabama slaves who took part in the Great Migration, to the steel mills of Gary, Indiana, to worldwide success, performing before the world's royalty, and honored by numerous heads of state. In contraposition, this family has suffered family division, divorce, scandal and other adversities, both business and personal, all magnified for public consumption.

The one family member who was under the microscope more than any other was the seventh son. Michael Jackson experienced turmoil after turmoil from a young age up to his 50th year and surprisingly he internally found the meeting place between child and man. The child was necessary to keep the turmoil from breaking him down and that required an innate strength. Jackson was not a weak man; the strength he possessed was that he inherited from his father. The album of his professional climax was not an album that broke through by accident in 1983; it was years in the making.

The years of 1975 to 1982 would be tempestuous years for Michael Jackson. This seven-year period would form the foundation from which all his energies would flow to create the biggest selling album of all time that became known as *Thriller*. The experiences and emotional hardships of this time would be channeled into present and future music. Through this determination, he was going to make it to the top of his profession.

Michael Jackson once said,

If you just went by blood, I'd have as much crane operator in me as singer.[cxxviii]

He also testified,

I have rhinoceros skin, but at the same time I'm human. So, anything can hurt but I'm very strong.[cxxix]

His fate, birthed from his personal destiny, was to be his own man, to separate himself from a family paradigm that stunted and stifled him both personally and creatively. He found and embraced his true self despite the opinions of critics and haters. Even in death, "Jack" is still…trying to make you happy from the legacy he left behind.

Once, it was written, "all children, except one, grow up."[cxxx] Now, it appears that all children mature when reaching their destiny.

Secretly and privately . . . really deep within there is a Destiny.

>   --Michael Joesph Jackson
>   Encino, California
>   December 1979

Works Cited

1. American Musicological Society. Best Practices In The Fair Use of Copyrighted Materials In Music Scholarship. AMS Directory 2010 (ISSN 1099-6796), pp. li-lv. Copyright © 2010 By The American Musicological Society, Inc. All Rights Reserved.

2. McInnis, C. Liegh. *The Lyrics of Prince Rogers Nelson: A Literary Look at a Creative, Musical Poet, Philosopher, and Storyteller.* Jackson: Psychedelic Literature, 2007. Print.

3. Bourasaw, Noel V. *"Go West, Young Man Who wrote it? Greeley or Soule?"* Skagit River Journal. Aug, 2016. http://www.skagitriverjournal.com/us/library/newspapers/greeley1-gowest.html

4. Weeks, William Earl. *Building the continental empire: American expansion from the Revolution to the Civil War.* Chicago: Ivan R. Dee. 1996. Print.

5. Lincoln, C. Eric. *The American Protest Movement for Negro Rights. The American Negro Reference Book.* Davis, John P., Seventh Printing, Prentice-Hall, September 1969, Englewood Cliffs, pp. 467.

6. In Motion: The African-American Migration Experience. *The Great Migration.* The Schomburg Center for Research in Black Culture. Aug, 2016. Web. http://www.inmotionaame.org/print.cfm;jsessionid=f8301628661472148378483?migration=8&bhcp=1

7. Hine, Darlene; Hine, William; Harrold, Stanley (2012). *African Americans: A Concise History* (4th ed.). Pearson Education, Inc., 2012, Boston, pp. 388–389.

8. Thornbrough, Emma Lou. *The Negro In Indiana: The Study of a Minority, Vol. 37.* Indianapolis: Indiana Historical Bureau, 1957. p. 392

9. Zulkin, Sharon. *Landscapes of Power: From Detroit to Disney World.* Berkeley: University of California Press, 1991. p. 60.

10. Taraborrelli, J. Randy. *Michael Jackson: The Magic and the Madness.* Seacaucus: Carol Publishing Group, 1991. Print.

11. Knopper, Steve. *The Genius of Michael Jackson.* New York: Scribner, 2015. Print.

12. Jackson, Katherine; Wiseman, Richard. *My Family, the Jacksons.* St. Martin's Paperbacks. 1990. New York.

13. Biography.com editors. "Joseph Jackson Biography." The Biography.com website. A&E Television Networks. June, 2016. Web.

14. Jackson, Michael. *Moonwalk.* New York: Doubleday, 1988. Print.

15. "Jackson 5 discography." Wikipedia: The Free Encyclopedia. Wikimedia Foundation, Inc. June, 2009. Web.

16. The Jacksons "Blues Away." Composed by Jackson, Michael Joe. *The Jacksons.* CBS-Epic/Philadelphia International: New York, 1976. Vinyl

17. Scott, JG, Cohen, D, DiCicco-Bloom B, Miller, W.L., Stange, K.C., Crabtree, B.F., *Understanding Healing Relationships In Primary Care.* Ann Fam Med. 2008; 6 [4]: 315-322.

18. The Jacksons "Style of Life." Composed by Jackson, Toriano Adaryll, Jackson, Michael Joe. The Jacksons.

CBS-Epic/Philadelphia International: New York, 1976. Vinyl.

19. The Jackson 5 "I'll Be There" composed by Gordy, Berry, Davis, Hal, West, Bob, Hutch, Willie. *Third Album.* Motown: Los Angeles, 1970. Vinyl.

20. *The Michael Jackson Story.* Director: Steve Cole, Perfs: Latoya Jackson, Suzanne DePasse, Liza Minnelli. Iambic Media Distributors: Independent Television (ITV), 2003.

21. "List of Concert Tours by Michael Jackson and the Jackson 5." *Wikipedia: The Free Encyclopedia.* Wikimedia Foundation, Inc. June, 2009. Web.

22. Discoguy. "This is Michael 'Mick' Jackson." *Disco-Disco.com.* Discoguy Productions. March 30, 2016. Web.

23. The Jacksons "Blame It On The Boogie." Composed by Jackson, Mick, Jackson, Dave, Krohn, Elmar. *Destiny.* CBS-Epic: New York, 1978. Compact Disc.

24. Steblin, Rita. *A History of Key Characteristics in the 18th and Early 19th Centuries.* Ann Arbor: UMI Research Press, 1983. Print.

25. The Jacksons "Push Me Away." Composed by Jackson, Toriano Adaryll, Jackson, Sigmund Esco, Jackson, Marlon David, Jackson, Michael Joesph, Jackson, Steven Randall. Destiny. CBS-Epic: New York, 1978. Compact Disc.

26. "Don Cornelius interviews Michael Jackson." Soul Train. You Tube. Perfs: Don Cornelius, Soul Train Dancers, The Jacksons. Don Cornelius Productions, 1979. Web.

27. The Jacksons. "Things I Do For You." Composed by Jackson, Toriano Adaryll, Jackson, Sigmund Esco, Jackson, Marlon David, Jackson, Michael Joesph, Jackson, Steven Randall. *Destiny.* CBS-Epic: New York, 1978. Compact Disc.

28. "Characteristics of Musical Keys." Biteyourownelbow.com. June, 2010. Web.

29. "The Hot 100: The Week of November 15, 1980. Billboard.com. March 30, 2016. Web.

30.   "Shake Your Body (Down To The Ground)." Composed by Jackson, Steven Randall, Jackson, Michael Joseph. *Destiny*. CBS-Epic: New York, 1978. Compact Disc.

31.   "WBLS Frankie Crocker's Interview with Michael Jackson at age 21." You Tube. Perfs: Frankie Crocker, Michael Jackson WBLS Radio New York 107.5 FM. Web.

32.   The Jacksons, Luongo, John. "Shake Your Body (Down To The Ground) REMIX. Composed by Jackson, Steven Randall, Jackson, Michael Joseph. Remixed and Edited by Luongo, John. 12" Maxi Single." June, 2010. Mp3.

33.   "Hot R&B/Hip-Hop Songs: The Week of April 21, 1979." Billboard.com. March 30, 2016. Web.

34.   "Artists/The Jacksons." Billboard.com. March 30, 2016. Web.

35.   "Gold & Platinum." Record Industry Association of America. RIAA.com. http://www.riaa.com/gold-platinum/?tab_active=default-award&ar=The+Jacksons&ti=Shake+Your+Body#search_section. March 30, 2016. Web.

36.   "The Jackson 5." *Wikipedia: The Free Encyclopedia.* Wikimedia Foundation, Inc. June, 2009. Web.

37.   The Jacksons. "Destiny." Composed by Jackson, Toriano Adaryll, Jackson, Sigmund Esco, Jackson, Marlon David, Jackson, Michael Joseph, Jackson, Steven Randall. *Destiny.* CBS-Epic: New York, 1978. Compact Disc.

38.   The Jacksons. "Bless His Soul." Composed by Jackson, Toriano Adaryll, Jackson, Sigmund Esco, Jackson, Marlon, David, Jackson, Michael Joesph, Jackson, Steven Randall. *Destiny.* CBS-Epic: New York, 1978. Compact Disc.

39.   Jackson, Michael, "The Dance." Poem, liner notes, *Dangerous.* Sony, 1991. Compact Disc.

40.   "Michael Jackson rare Interview with Merv Griffin Jackson 5." You Tube. Perfs: Merv Griffin, Michael Jackson, The Jackson 5. Merv Griffin Productions, 1974. Web.

41.   "Michael Jackson Studio 54 Interview." You Tube. Perfs: Steve Rubell, Michael Jackson, Jane Pauley,

Liza Minnelli. Iounis Productions, 1977. Web.

42. Holiday, Billie. "T'aint Nobody's Business If I Do." Composed by Grainger, Porter, Robbins, Everett. Billie Holiday's Greatest Hits. MCA: Universal City, 1980. Cassette.

43. *Jazz*, Director: Ken Burns, Perfs. Louis Armstrong, Duke Ellington, Miles Davis. Florentine Films, WETA, PBS, 2001.

44. The Jacksons. "That's What You Get For Being Polite." Composed by Jackson, Toriano Adaryll, Jackson, Sigmund Esco, Jackson, Marlon, Jackson, Michael Joesph, Jackson, Steven Randall. Destiny. CBS-Epic: New York, 1978. Compact Disc.

45. Robert E. Johnson, "The Michael Jackson Nobody Knows," Ebony, December, 1984, 155.

46. Harriet Cole, "Michael Jackson: Then & Now," Ebony, December, 2007, 80.

47. Jeans, Sir. James. Science & Music. Chapter V Harmony & Discord, Key Characteristics. Internet Archive Wayback Machine.

http://web.archive.org/web/2005041916 2711/http://www.win.net/~pelerin/music/science/music5.html March, 30, 2016. Web.

48. Access Hollywood. "Michael Jackson: Access Hollywood Special/"Blue Gangsta" Snippet." Online video clip. YouTube. YouTube, 13 Apr. 2009. Web. 4 Oct. 2013.

49. The Artful Mind: Cognitive Science and the Riddle of Human Creativity. Ed. Mark Turner. Oxford: Oxford University Press, 2006. Print.

50. O'Toole, Kit. Michael Jackson FAQ: All That's Left To Know About The King Of Pop, Milwaukee, Backbeat, 2015. Print.

51. The Jacksons, Destiny, Perfs: Tito Jackson, Jackie Jackson, Marlon Jackson, Michael Jackson, Randy Jackson. Dec. 1978. Vinyl.

52. "Blank on Blank-Michael Jackson on Godliness." blankonblank.org, January, 1980. http://blankon blank.org/interviews/michael-jackson-godliness 13 July 2016. Web.

53. Michael Jackson's Journey: From Motown To Off The Wall. Dir. Spike Lee. Perfs: Michael Jackson, Jackson 5, Berry

Gordy, Suzanne De Passe, Katherine Jackson. Showtime, 2016. Film.

54. Rivera, Geraldo (Interviewer) & Jackson, Michael (Interviewee). 2005. At Large With Geraldo Rivera Interview (Feb 2005). Retrieved from ALL MICHAEL JACKSON.com: http://www.allmichaeljackson.com/interviews/geraldorivera.html

55. Barrie, James Matthew. Peter And Wendy. Illus. Francis Donkin Bedford. New York: Charles Scribner & Sons. 1911. Print.

56. "Destiny World Tour." Wikipedia: The Free Encyclopedia. Wikimedia Foundation, Inc. July 15, 2016. Web.

APPENDIX

Industry Chart Figures of The Jacksons' *Destiny*

Billboard Singles

"Blame It On The Boogie"	Released October 23, 1978 R&B Singles Chart........3 Billboard Hot 100.........54
"Shake Your Body (Down To the Ground)"	Released February 10, 1979 R&B Singles Chart........3 Billboard Hot 100...........7
"Destiny"	Released May 11, 1979 *Did not chart in the U.S. but reached #39 in the U.K. singles chart.

Billboard Albums

"Destiny"	R&B Albums Chart.......3 Billboard 200...............11

The Destiny World Tour

Destiny Tour Poster - Author's Collection

The Destiny World Tour was the first world tour for The Jacksons after signing with

CBS records three years earlier. The tour was in support of their masterpiece, the Destiny album. The tour began on January 22, 1979 in Bremen, Germany, just four weeks after the release of the album the previous December. The tour visited three continents, nine countries, playing 83 cities in the United States alone. The first leg of the tour, The Jacksons performed in moderate sized arenas that seated 3,000 and slightly more. Afterwards, there was a four-month break in the tour so that Michael Jackson could finish work on his solo Epic debut release, *Off The Wall*.

After the release of the album and the positive reception from the critics and the public, the brothers were forced to revamp the show play larger arenas, like the like the Philadelphia Spectrum which seats 16,000. Songs from the *Off The Wall* album were added to the second leg of the tour and an opening act was added, L.T.D. The tour earned 7.5 million dollars[cxxxi].

First Leg (1979) SET LIST
1. "Dancing Machine"
2. "Things I Do for You"
3. "Ben"
4. "Keep on Dancing"
5. Jackson 5 Medley:
"I Want You Back"/"ABC"/"The Love You Save"/
"I'll Be There"
6. "Band Introduction"
7. "Enjoy Yourself"
8. "Destiny"

9. "Show You The Way To Go"
10. "All Night Dancin'"
11. "Blame It On The Boogie"

Second & Third Leg (1979-1980) SET LIST

1. "Dancing Machine"

2. "Things I Do for You"

3. "Ben"

4. "Off the Wall"

5. Jackson 5 Medley:

"I Want You Back"/"ABC"/"The Love You Save"/"I'll Be There"

6. "Rock With You"

7. "Blame It On The Boogie"

8. "Don't Stop 'Til You Get Enough"

9. "Shake Your Body (Down To The Ground)"

Personnel

- Michael Jackson: Lead Vocals

- Jackie Jackson: Vocals

- Tito Jackson: Guitar, Vocals

- Marlon Jackson: Vocals

- Randy Jackson: Vocals, Congas, Percussion, Piano, Keyboards

Band Members

First Leg

- Bass: Michael McKinney

- Additional Guitar: Bud Rizzo

- Keyboards: James Macfield

- Drums: Tony Lewis

Second and Third Leg

- Drums: Jonathan Moffett

- Additional Guitar: Bud Rizzo

- Bass: Michael McKinney

- Keyboards: James Macfield

- Horns: (East Coast Horns): Wesley Phillips, Cloris Grimes, Alan (Funt) Prater, Roderick (Mac) McMorris

Tour Dates

Europe		
January 22-24-26, 1979	Bremen, Germany	Wilheim Kaisen Platz
January 27, 1979	Frankfurt, Germany	Festhalle Frankfurt
January 28-29-30, 1979	Madrid, Spain	Teatro Monumental
February 1-2, 1979	Amsterdam, Netherlands	Koninklijk Theater Carre
February 6-7-8-9, 1979	London, England, United Kingdom	Rainbow Theatre
February 10, 1979	Brighton, England, United Kingdom	Top Rank

February 11, 1979	Preston, Lancashire, England, United Kingdom	Preston Guild Hall
February 12, 1979	Wakefield, West Yorkshire, England, United Kingdom	Theatre Royal
February 13, 1979	Sheffield, South, Yorkshire, England, United Kingdom	Fiesta Nightclub
February 14-15, 1979	Geneva, Switzerland	Victoria Hall (Victoria)
February 16, 1979	Glasgow, Scotland, United Kingdom	Glasgow Apollo
February 17, 1979	Manchester England, United Kingdom	Manchester Apollo
February 18, 1979	Birmingham England, United Kingdom	Bingley Hall

February 19, 1979	Leeds, West Yorkshire, England, United Kingdom	Queens Hall
February 20, 1979	Leicester, England, United Kingdom	DeMontfort Hall
February 21, 1979	Cardiff, Wales	Sophia Gardens Pavillion
February 23-24, 1979	London, England,	Rainbow Theatre
February 25, 1979	Poole, England	Pavillion Theatre
February 26, 1979	Amsterdam, Netherlands	Concertgebouw
February 29, 1979	Avignon, France	Théâtre des Cermes
March 2, 1979	Paris, France	Le Palace

Africa		
March 6-7-8-9-10, 1979	Johannesburg, South Africa	Orlando Stadium
March 12-13-14-15, 1979	Dakar, Senegal	Stade de l'Amitié
March 16-17, 1979	Capetown, South Africa	Green Point Stadium
March 19-20-21, 1979	Johannesburg, South Africa	Orlando Stadium

North America – First Leg

Date	Location	Venue
April 14-15, 1979	Cleveland, Ohio, United States	Music Hall
April 19, 22, 1979	Valley Forge, Pennsylvania, United States	Valley Forge Music Fair
April 25-26-27, 29, 1979	Chicago, Illinois, United States	Arie Crown Theater
May 3, 1979	St. Petersburg, Florida, United States	Bayfront Center
May 4, 1979	Fort Pierce, Florida, United States	Unknown Venue
May 6, 1979	Jacksonville, Florida, United States	Jacksonville Memorial Coliseum
May 10, 12, 1979	Houston, Texas, United States	Houston Music Hall
May 16, 1979	Birmingham, Alabama, United States	Birmingham-Jefferson Civic Center Coliseum
May 17, 1979	Columbus, Ohio, United States	Municipal Auditorium

May 18, 1979	Nashville, Tennessee, United States	War Memorial Auditorium
May 19, 1979	Atlanta, Georgia, United States	Atlanta Civic Center
May 20, 1979	Memphis, Tennessee, United States	Orpheum Theatre
May 24, 1979	Pine Bluff, Arkansas, United States	Pine Bluff Convention Center
May 26, 1979	Kansas City, Missouri, United States	Municipal Auditorium
May 27, 1979	Oklahoma City, Oklahoma, United States	Fairgrounds Arena
May 30, 1979	Shreveport, Louisiana, United States	Hirsch Memorial Coliseum
June 1, 1979	Norfolk, Virginia, United States	The Scope
June 3, 1979	Columbia, South Carolina, United States	Carolina Coliseum
June 8, 1979	Charlotte, North Carolina, United States	Charlotte Coliseum

June 9, 1979	Landover, Maryland, United States	Capital Centre
June 10, 1979	Greensboro, North Carolina, United States	War Memorial Auditorium

North America – Second Leg		
September 26, 1979	Washington, D.C., United States	RFK Memorial Stadium
October 2-3, 1979	New Orleans, Louisiana, United States	Municipal Auditorium
October 4, 1979	Shreveport, Louisiana, United States	Hirsch Memorial Coliseum
October 5, 1979	Mobile, Alabama, United States	Municipal Auditorium
October 6, 1979	Huntsville, Alabama, United States	Von Braun Civic Center
October 7, 1979	Louisville, Kentucky, United States	Louisville Gardens
October 12, 1979	Philadelphia, Pennsylvania, United States	The Spectrum
October 13, 1979	Rochester, New York, United States	Rochester Community War Memorial

October 14, 1979	Pittsburgh, Pennsylvania, United States	Civic Arena
October 15, 1979	Saginaw, Michigan, United States	Saginaw Civic Center
October 19, 1979	Indianapolis, Indiana, United States	Market Square Arena
October 20, 1979	St. Louis, Missouri, United States	Kiel Auditorium
October 21, 1979	Dayton, Ohio, United States	University of Dayton Arena
October 25, 1979	Columbus, Ohio, United States	Fairground Coliseum
October 26, 1979	Syracuse, New York, United States	War Memorial Auditorium
October 27, 1979	Buffalo, New York, United States	Buffalo Memorial Auditorium
October 28, 1979	Springfield, Massachusetts, United States	Civic Center
November 1, 1979	Kalamazoo, Michigan, United States	Wings Stadium
November 2, 1979	Chicago, Illinois, United States	Chicago Stadium
November 3, 1979	Cleveland, Ohio, United States	Convention Centre

November 4-5, 1979	Detroit, Michigan, United States	Cobo Hall
November 6, 1979	Baltimore, Maryland, United States	Civic Center
November 8, 1979	Richmond, Virginia, United States	Richmond Coliseum
November 9, 1979	Hampstead, New York, United States	Nassau Coliseum
November 10, 1979	Hampton, Virginia, United States	Hampton Coliseum
November 11, 1979	Fayetteville, North Carolina, United States	Cumberland County Auditorium
November 14, 1979	Fort Worth, Texas, United States	Tarrant County Convention Center
November 15, 1979	Baton Rouge, Louisiana, United States	Riverside Centroplex
November 16, 1979	Jackson, Mississippi, United States	Jackson Coliseum
November 17, 1979	Lake Charles, Louisiana, United States	Civic Center
November 18-19, 2017	Houston, Texas, United States	The Summit

November 20, 1979	Columbus, Georgia, United States	Municipal Auditorium
November 21, 1979	Greenville, South Carolina, United States	Greenville Auditorium
November 22, 1979	Savannah, Georgia, United States	Civic Center
November 23, 1979	Macon, Georgia, United States	Macon Coliseum
November 24, 1979	Nashville, Tennessee, United States	Nashville Municipal Auditorium
November 25, 1979	Atlanta, Georgia, United States	The Omni
November 29, 1979	Albuquerque, New Mexico, United States	University Arena
November 30, 1979	Denver, Colorado, United States	McNichols Sports Arena
December 2, 1979	Honolulu, Hawaii, United States	Neal Blaisdell Center
December 6, 1979	Portland, Oregon, United States	Memorial Coliseum
December 8, 1979	Seattle, Washington, United States	Seattle Center Coliseum

December 9, 1979	Vancouver, British Columbia, Canada	Pacific National Exhibition A.R.
December 13, 1979	San Bernardino, California, United States	Swing Auditorium
December 14, 1979	Phoenix, Arizona, United States	Arizona Veterans Memorial Coliseum
December 15, 1979	San Diego, California, United States	San Diego Sports Arena
December 16, 1979	Oakland, California, United States	Oakland Coliseum
December 18, 1979	Inglewood, California, United States	The Forum
December 21, 1979	Nassau, New Providence, The Bahamas	Haynes Oval

North America – Third Leg		
September 5, 1980	Honolulu, Hawaii, United States	Neal Blaisdell Center
September 17-18-19-25-26, 1980	Inglewood, California, United States	The Forum

Television Appearances		
January 25, 1979	Musikladen (Radio Bremen Germany)	Song(s) Performed: "Blame It On The Boogie"
February 2, 1979	The Midnight Special (NBC)	"Shake Your Body (Down To the Ground)" "Destiny" "Things I Do For You" "Shake Your Body (Down To The Ground)"
February 3, 1979	Soul Train (Tribune Entertainment)	"Things I Do For You" "Shake Your Body (Down To The Ground)" "Blame It On The Boogie" (Music Video) "Push Me Away" (Michael Jackson, solo)

| February 10, 1979 | American Bandstand (ABC) | "Shake Your Body (Down To The Ground)" "Push Me Away" (Michael Jackson, solo) "Things I Do For You" |

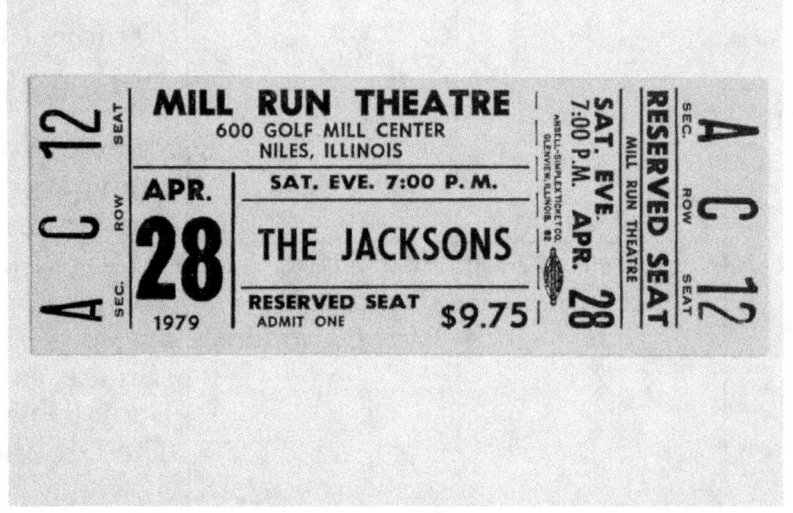

Original Destiny *tour ticket for The Jacksons, April 28, 1979, Mill Run Theatre - Author's Collection*

About the Author

The author in front of The Jackson Family home in Gary, Indiana

L. Roi Boyd, III is a Professor of Speech and Theatre at Virginia State University, Virginia Union University and an adjunct Professor of Mass Communications at Virginia Commonwealth University. He received his MFA degree from Virginia Commonwealth in 2002 in Theatre Pedagogy. He is a Professor, Guitarist, Drummer, and Actor; he has been teaching and directing in educational, community, and professional theatre for nearly 25 years in Virginia and North Carolina. He is a historian in

African American Film history specializing in Race movies and Blaxploitation film. Boyd is also a filmmaker, having directed the RLP Productions film "Bell Blu" in 2008. In addition, he served as co-producer of the film "Black Wall Street: The Money, The Music, The People." in addition to co-writing the theme song to the movie. Boyd serves as Co-Founding Artistic director of Cultural Libations, a multidisciplinary arts & humanities company.

As a scholar, Roi has presented research and moderated panels for The Black Theatre Network, The Southern Theatre Conference, and the Culturing The Popular Conference. As a Director, his work has been in produced in Norfolk, Richmond, Winston Salem, North Carolina, San Francisco and New York City. Boyd has been following the careers of The Jacksons and Michael Jackson for 44 years. He is an avid collector of pop culture and Jackson memorabilia for nearly 35 years. Roi and his life partner, Yemaja Jubilee, divide their time between Richmond and Charlotte County, VA.

About the Cover Artist

Martha Harvin, better known to the world as Martha High, has a singing career that began with the Jewels. Noticed by "The Godfather of Soul," Mr. James Brown, Martha and The Jewels went on the road to perform with him in his famous James Brown Review. Martha remained with him for 32 years becoming the only female to have performed with him for that length of time.

Martha has also graced the stage with some of the greatest performers of our time including Michael Jackson, Bo Diddley, and BB King. Martha has also been featured in the movie "The Blues Brothers." With a career spanning five decades, she is a highly sought-after performer with five albums to her credit. She has just completed her first book, "He's a Funny Cat, Ms. High: My 32 years Singing with James Brown" with stories, funny and sad, that have never been told before. Today, Martha continues to grace the stage and delight audiences in Europe, Asia, and America.

Photography by Robert L. Sims, III

- 2300 Jackson Street (page 31)
- Jackson Brothers Mural (page 54)
- About the Author photograph (page 247)

Original Artwork by Martha High

- Teenager (page 38)
- Young Man (page 145)
- Downfall – The Agony (page 207)

Memorabilia Photography from the Author's Private Collection by Danny Holcomb

- "Blame It On The Boogie" 12 inch single (page 82)
- "Shake Your Body (Down To The Ground)" 12 inch single (page 119)
- "Bless His Soul" 45 rpm single (page 148)
- "This is It" Coin (front and back) (page 191)
- "Ebony" Magazine Ad (page 193)
- The Jackson Brothers at the recording console (page 197)
- Destiny Album Cover (page 198)
- Destiny Tour Programme (page 201)
- Destiny Tour Pin (page 204)
- Destiny Tour Poster (page 225)
- Destiny Tour Ticket (page 246)

[i] American Musicological Society. *Best Practices In The Fair Use of Copyrighted Materials In Music Scholarship.*
[ii] McInnis, C. Liegh. *The Lyrics of Prince Rogers Nelson: A Literary Look at a Creative, Musical Poet, Philosopher, and Storyteller.*
[iii] Bourasaw, Noel V. "Go West Young Man Who Wrote it? Greeley or Soule?"
[iv] Bourasaw, Noel V. "Go West Young Man Who Wrote it? Greeley or Soule?"
[v] Weeks, William Earl. *Building the continental empire: American expansion from the Revolution to the Civil War.*
[vi] Lincoln, C. Eric. *The American Protest Movement for Negro Rights. The American Negro Reference Book.*
[vii] In Motion: The African-American Migration Experience. *The Great Migration.*
[viii] Hine, Darlene; Hine, William; Harrold, Stanley (2012). *African-Americans: A Concise History.*
[ix] Thornbrough, Emma Lou. *The Negro in Indiana: The Study of a Minority, Vol 37.*
[x] Thornbrough, Emma Lou. *The Negro in Indiana: The Study of a Minority, Vol 37.*
[xi] Zulkin, Sharon. *Landscapes of Power: From Detroit to Disney World.*
[xii] Zulkin, Sharon. *Landscapes of Power: From Detroit to Disney World.*
[xiii] Taraborrelli, J. Randy. *Michael Jackson: The Magic and the Madness.*
[xiv] Taraborrelli, J. Randy. *Michael Jackson: The Magic and the Madness.*
[xv] Knopper, Steve. *The Genius of Michael Jackson.*
[xvi] Jackson, Katherine; Wiseman, Richard. *My Family, the Jacksons.*
[xvii] Biography.com editors. "Joseph Jackson Biography."
[xviii] Taraborrelli, J. Randy. *Michael Jackson: The Magic and the Madness.*
[xix] Knopper, Steve. *The Genius of Michael Jackson.*
[xx] Taraborrelli, J. Randy. *Michael Jackson: The Magic and the Madness.*
[xxi] Taraborrelli, J. Randy. *Michael Jackson: The Magic and the Madness.*
[xxii] Taraborrelli, J. Randy. *Michael Jackson: The Magic and the Madness.*
[xxiii] Jackson, Michael. *Moonwalk.*
[xxiv] Taraborrelli, J. Randy. *Michael Jackson: The Magic and the Madness.*
[xxv] Taraborrelli, J. Randy. *Michael Jackson: The Magic and the Madness.*
[xxvi] "Jackson 5 Discography" Wikipedia.
[xxvii] Jackson, Michael. *Moonwalk.*
[xxviii] Jackson, Michael. *Moonwalk.*
[xxix] The Jacksons "Blues Away."
[xxx] Jackson, Michael. *Moonwalk.*
[xxxi] Scott, J.G.; Cohen, D; DiCicco-Bloom B; Miller, W.L.; Stange, K.C.; Crabtree, B.F. *Understanding Healing Relationships in Primary Care.*
[xxxii] The Jacksons, "Style of Life."
[xxxiii] The Jackson 5, "I'll Be There."
[xxxiv] Jackson, Michael. *Moonwalk.*
[xxxv] Jackson, Michael. *Moonwalk.*
[xxxvi] Taraborrelli, J. Randy. *Michael Jackson: The Magic and the Madness.*
[xxxvii] Jackson, Michael. *Moonwalk.*
[xxxviii] Jackson, Michael. *Moonwalk.*
[xxxix] Jackson, Michael. *Moonwalk.*

xl *The Michael Jackson Story*. Director: Steve Cole
xli Taraborrelli, J. Randy. *Michael Jackson: The Magic and the Madness*.
xlii Taraborrelli, J. Randy. *Michael Jackson: The Magic and the Madness*.
xliii "List of Concert Tours by Michael Jackson and the Jackson 5." Wikipedia.
xliv Jackson, Michael. *Moonwalk*.
xlv "Jackson 5 Discography" Wikipedia.
xlvi "Jackson 5 Discography" Wikipedia.
xlvii Jackson, Michael. *Moonwalk*.
xlviii Discoguy. "This is Michael 'Mick' Jackson."
xlix Discoguy. "This is Michael 'Mick' Jackson."
l The Jacksons, "Blame It On the Boogie."
li The Jacksons, "Blame It On the Boogie."
lii The Jacksons, "Blame It On the Boogie."
liii The Jacksons, "Blame It On the Boogie."
liv Taraborrelli, J. Randy. *Michael Jackson: The Magic and the Madness*.
lv Jackson, Michael. *Moonwalk*.
lvi Steblin, Rita. *A History of Key Characteristics in the 18th and Early 19th Centuries*.
lvii The Jacksons, "Push Me Away."
lviii Jackson, Michael. *Moonwalk*.
lix The Jacksons, "Push Me Away."
lx The Jacksons, "Push Me Away."
lxi The Jacksons, "Push Me Away."
lxii The Jacksons, "Push Me Away."
lxiii Taraborrelli, J. Randy. *Michael Jackson: The Magic and the Madness*.
lxiv Knopper, Steve. *The Genius of Michael Jackson*.
lxv Jackson, Michael. *Moonwalk*.
lxvi Jackson, Michael. *Moonwalk*.
lxvii The Jacksons, "Things I Do For You."
lxviii The Jacksons, "Things I Do For You."
lxix The Jacksons, "Things I Do For You."
lxx The Jacksons, "Things I Do For You."
lxxi "Characteristics of Musical Keys." Biteyourownelbow.com
lxxii Knopper, Steve. *The Genius of Michael Jackson*.
lxxiii Knopper, Steve. *The Genius of Michael Jackson*.
lxxiv "The Hot 100: The Week of November 15, 1980."
lxxv Jackson, Steven Randall; Jackson, Michael. "Shake Your Body Down To The Ground."
lxxvi "WBLS Frankie Crocker's Interview with Michael Jackson at age 21." YouTube.
lxxvii Jackson, Steven Randall; Jackson, Michael. "Shake Your Body Down To The Ground."
lxxviii The Jacksons; Luongo, John. "Shake Your Body (Down To The Ground) REMIX.
lxxix "Hot R&B/Hip-Hop Songs: The Week of April 21, 1979."
lxxx "Artists/The Jacksons."
lxxxi "Gold & Platinum" Record Industry Association of America.
lxxxii "The Jackson 5." Wikipedia.
lxxxiii The Jacksons, "Destiny."
lxxxiv The Jacksons, "Destiny."
lxxxv The Jacksons, "Destiny."
lxxxvi Jackson, Michael. *Moonwalk*.
lxxxvii Jackson, Michael. *Moonwalk*.
lxxxviii The Jacksons, "Destiny."
lxxxix The Jacksons, "Destiny."
xc The Jacksons, "Bless His Soul."
xci Jackson, Michael. *Moonwalk*.
xcii The Jacksons, "Bless His Soul."
xciii "The Jackson 5." Wikipedia.
xciv Jackson, Michael. "The Dance."
xcv "Michael Jackson rare interview with Merv Griffin Jackson 5" YouTube.

xcvi "Michael Jackson rare interview with Merv Griffin Jackson 5" YouTube.
xcvii "Michael Jackson rare interview with Merv Griffin Jackson 5" YouTube.
xcviii Holliday, Billie. "T'aint Nobody's Business If I Do."
xcix The Jacksons, "All Night Dancin'"
c *Jazz*, Director: Ken Burns.
ci The Jacksons. "That's What You Get For Being Polite."
cii The Jacksons. "That's What You Get For Being Polite."
ciii The Jacksons. "That's What You Get For Being Polite."
civ The Jacksons. "That's What You Get For Being Polite."
cv The Jacksons. "That's What You Get For Being Polite."
cvi The Jacksons. "That's What You Get For Being Polite."
cvii The Jacksons. "That's What You Get For Being Polite."
cviii The Jacksons. "That's What You Get For Being Polite."
cix Johnson, Robert E. "The Michael Jackson Nobody Knows."
cx Cole, Harriet. "Michael Jackson: Then & Now."
cxi Jackson, Michael. *Moonwalk*.
cxii Jean, Sir James. *Science and Music*.
cxiii Access Hollywood. "Michael Jackson: Access Hollywood Special/"Blue Gangsta" Snippet."
cxiv The Artful Mind: Cognitive Science and the Riddle of Human Creativity.
cxv Taraborrelli, J. Randy. *Michael Jackson: The Magic and the Madness*.
cxvi Taraborrelli, J. Randy. *Michael Jackson: The Magic and the Madness*.
cxvii TMZ.com, "Paul Anka - - 'Honest Mistake'", http://www.tmz.com/2009/10/12/paul-anka-michael-jackson-this-is-it-publishing-rigts/, 10/12/2009 9:10 PM PDT
cxviii TMZ.com, "Paul Anka - - 'Honest Mistake'", http://www.tmz.com/2009/10/12/paul-anka-michael-jackson-this-is-it-publishing-rigts/, 10/12/2009 9:10 PM PDT
cxix Taraborrelli, J. Randy. *Michael Jackson: The Magic and the Madness*.
cxx Access Hollywood. "Michael Jackson: Access Hollywood Special/"Blue Gangsta" Snippet."
cxxi Brown, Geoff. *Michael Jackson*.
cxxii O'Toole, Kit. *Michael Jackson FAQ*.
cxxiii The Jacksons. *Destiny*.
cxxiv "Blank on Blank – Michael Jackson on Godliness."
cxxv *Michael Jackson's Journey: From Motown to Off The Wall* Director: Spike Lee.
cxxvi *Michael Jackson's Journey: From Motown to Off The Wall* Director: Spike Lee.
cxxvii *Michael Jackson's Journey: From Motown to Off The Wall* Director: Spike Lee.
cxxviii Rivera, Geraldo & Jackson, Michael. "At Large with Geraldo Rivera" Interview.
cxxix Rivera, Geraldo & Jackson, Michael. "At Large with Geraldo Rivera" Interview.
cxxx Barrie, James Matthew. *Peter and Wendy*.
cxxxi Johnson, Robert E. "The Michael Jackson Nobody Knows."

www.ingramcontent.com/pod-product-compliance
Lightning Source LLC
LaVergne TN
LVHW051545070426
835507LV00021B/2414